The
SIMPLICITY
PROJECT

A SIMPLE, NO-NONSENSE
APPROACH TO LOSING WEIGHT
& CHANGING YOUR BODY

Forever!

Jenn Pike

www.simplicityyoga.ca

TESTIMONIALS

"The Simplicity Project is a masterful compilation of everything you could possibly want to know if you'd like to create a healthier, lighter, more vital version of yourself. I've known Jenn for years and I can tell you that she embodies these very concepts you're about to read.

Professionally, I have referred hundreds of patients to her services as a Registered Holistic Nutritionist because of her phenomenal ability to communicate complex ideas in a simple, specific and realistic manner. She knows it's not enough for you to just receive the information, but to know *how* it fits into your life and is going to result in lasting changes.

Jenn's heart, passion, humour and say-it-like-it-is approach is 100% refreshing. She is your biggest cheerleader and your most blunt friend all rolled into one! Enjoy this book—it will most certainly change your life if you let it."

Dr. Laura Foster, D.C., B.Sc.

"Jenn Pike is my go-to resource for nutritional education and combined physical therapies. Her extensive qualifications and experience, and her boundless enthusiasm, provide us all with the information and motivation we need to improve our health and well-being."

My Light to Your Light, Tathaastu* SO BE IT,
Theresa Gagnon

"I am not a person who is partial to testimonials in general, but my exposure to, and involvement with Jenn Pike and Simplicity have been life-changing for me, therefore, I would like to share my experience with others.

I met Jenn when she first opened up Simplicity in 2010. I was 57 at the time, had exercised all my life, but needed something else in my life. I had recently retired from a career with the Ontario Public Service and was going through 'new retiree' doubts. I hadn't practiced yoga in a very long time, but had this nagging pull to go back and revisit it. So I took the plunge.

What has inspired and kept me loyal to Jenn Pike and Simplicity? Simple. It's her vision, her energetic personality, her caring, and understanding. The studio itself is a thriving mini hamlet of yoga, health, wellness and friendship. I find it inspirational, soothing, and above all, my second home. My immersion into yoga and all it encompasses has helped me become a more understanding, calm and nurturing individual. I eat and live healthier!

Jenn has shown me what is possible at any age and, as a result, I have learned to enjoy life more, accept and address challenges as they arise and appreciate everyone in my life. My objective is to emulate Jenn's focus and passion and become a yoga teacher myself in one year's time.

I truly respect Jenn and all the personal sacrifices she has made to make her dream come true! We in the community have definitely benefited greatly!

Here's to your continued passion, health and growth!"

Hugs, Sandy Wickeler

"I met Jenn Pike almost two years ago when I walked into her yoga studio with the intention to introduce a new component to my exercise practice—stretching. I'd never done much of it before. My intention was that simple when I first went there—I needed to start stretching. Now, almost two years later, my life has gone through a major transformation. Jenn has been my yoga instructor, my personal trainer, my nutritionist, an invaluable consultant, a great inspiration, and an exceptional role model. Jenn leads the way for, and motivates people to take control of their body, mind and health. And what I love about Jenn's style is she is practical, real and down to earth. I am personally inspired by Jenn's example to be the best me and have fun doing it!"

Heidi McDonald

"The practice of holistic nutrition is an incredible science of combination and observation. Jenn has an outstanding talent and the wisdom to support the best balanced and complete program for her students. She is an advocate of empowerment and education. She is exceptional in her approach to the best potential and, most importantly, Jenn demonstrates a total holistic lifestyle. She is an active, wise and truthful model of her beliefs in action. Thanks Jenn. You inspire me!"

Ann Green

Library and Archives Canada Cataloguing in Publication

The Simplicity Project
Jenn Pike

Paperback ISBN 978-0-9917530-2-4

e-book: 978-0-9917530-4-8
e-reader: 978-0-9917530-3-1

Although the author and publisher have made every effort to
ensure that the information in this book was correct at press
time, the author and publisher do not assume and hereby dis-
claim any liability to any party for any loss, damage, or disruption
caused by errors or omissions, whether such errors or omissions
result from negligence, accident, or any other cause.

Editing, Proofing, Publishing: I C Publishing
Design and Layout: WeMakeBooks.ca

Printed in Canada
ICpublishing.ca

TABLE OF CONTENTS

Chapter 1

IGNITE THE FIRE WITHIN

Chapter 2

TO GET OUT OF YOUR RUT, YOU'VE GOT TO START WITH YOUR GUT

Chapter 3

YOUR FOOD. YOUR MOOD. YOUR ATTITUDE.

Chapter 4

FANNING THE OUT-OF-CONTROL FLAMES—GETTING RID OF INFLAMMATION

Chapter 5

GETTING STARTED

Chapter 6

GETTING EXCITED FOR
WHAT'S ON THE MENU

Chapter 7

CREATING THE BODY YOU WANT FOR LIFE

Chapter 8

SIMPLIFYING SUPPLEMENTS— AN INTEGRAL PART OF YOUR PROJECT!

Chapter 9

TREATING YOUR WHOLE BODY LIKE A GODDESS

Chapter 10

LET THE JOURNEY BEGIN

FOREWORD

I first met Jenn Pike in a yoga workshop I was leading in Canada. She'd had the guts to postpone her own studio opening for a few days in order to attend and sit with someone she felt might have some inspiration for her. That's when I knew I liked this woman.

It wasn't until we began talking after class, and her incredible depth of nutrition and fitness knowledge came pouring out that I understood that I needed her as well.

I've become an international yoga and wellness instructor, TV host, author, and much more. Along with manifesting my personal and professional dreams, I'd been on a physical tear, constantly touring to teach, existing between airports and hotels, saying yes to every opportunity that was presented, and sometimes, neglecting my own self-nourishment in favour of just "getting it done". I was beginning to default to sugary lattes and quick-fixes to power me through.

One day I was feeling so fatigued and bloated after an especially long time on the road—and eating poorly. I knew I needed to do something differently, after all, I am a role model for health, so I had to rein it in, not only for my own sake, but so that I could speak in public to my students and not feel like a hypocrite.

Diet, or as I like to call it, a "food lifestyle" is personal, yet there are some principles that are absolutely universal. And when it comes to the Self, it's all too easy to lose perspective. I definitely had.

Jenn intervened, went through an entire nutrition profile for me and my activity level, and pinpointed many places, such as lack of enough protein and the aforementioned sugar addiction, where I was sabotaging, not supporting, all the good work I was doing out in the world—and in my body.

Together we were able to kick my negative habits to the curb and make space for me in the madness, all while keeping my best body-mind-spirit routines so simple—simple enough to fit into my busy life, and that's saying a lot.

Using Jenn's program, I lost excess weight and bloating, gained energy, and found that toned, true body I knew was in there somewhere. Best of all, I'm now empowered to clearly, straightforwardly understand how to carry this state of being through my whole life, forever. There is no better gift than this, and you are holding it in your hands.

And don't worry—there are so many different voices and opinions on what works when it comes to your health ... and at this point, I've probably met them all, or at least done their programs. I can tell you that Jenn is the real deal. Out of all the experts I've met, she is one of the few I could confidently categorize as a genius.

Yet somehow, she has simplified her genius so that anyone and everyone can grasp exactly what to do next to co-create their most incredible, vibrant experience, not of simply living, but of fully being *alive*.

For me, this is the mark of a masterful teacher: someone who not only knows things, but can translate them into practical tips and tools that anyone, from über-yogis to frazzled new moms, stressed execs and beyond can apply—today— with ease.

We require a lifestyle of giving out without burning out,

and Jenn's book, *The Simplicity Project* is your best advocate to transform yourself into the vital, glowing, fit, toned, energetic you that you're meant to be. I love her principles so much, I included some of Jenn's quick recipes, and *The Simplicity Project* as a resource in my own book, *The 21-Day Yoga Body* (Random House, Sept 2013).

I'm not only blessed to have Jenn as one of my colleagues and support network, I'm excited for you to gain the fast-track to the wisdom and techniques that she's compiled and simplified over the course of many years. Now you can skip light-years ahead; just follow the program, and watch yourself be revealed and renewed, on all levels.

I'll see you on the other side. It's incredible over here.

Sadie Nardini
Host of *Rock Your Yoga* on Viera Living TV
Author of the *21 Day Yoga Body* (Random House)

ACKNOWLEDGEMENTS AND GRATITUDE

I am so grateful for all of the amazing people, teachers, students and influences in my life; it is a challenge for me to summarize my appreciation to a few. First and foremost I need to thank my husband, Chris, who has been so supportive and loving during this whole journey, and our two amazing and spirited children, Emerson and Sam. They have, by far, been my greatest teachers in life and continue to push me to creative abilities I did not know I had. They are also, quite possibly, the best huggers. To my Mom and Dad, you have always been my biggest fans and made me feel like anything was possible. I have no doubt that growing up with home-cooked meals made the difference and guided me to where I am today. So much love to you both. To my sister, Wendy, my brother, Matthew, and their families, your love, enthusiasm and support mean the world to me. To Bruce, Lesley and kids, thank you for your support and never-ending excitement for all I do. And to my girlfriends, thank you for years of enduring my recommendations, classes and insane schedule. I love you all.

To MY teachers: Caroline Dupont, my earliest teachings in your kitchen and with your books sparked my interest in this field, which eventually led me to this point. Your kindness, passion, and integrity are absolutely infectious. Theresa Gagnon, you were by far the greatest influence in my yoga practice. Your teachings extended beyond the mat, and I am always grateful for you and our friendship. Ann Green, my friend, you are the truest warrior of life that I know! You are such an inspiration of growth, love, and real humanity; I cherish our friendship and look forward to future projects and endeavours together. Sadie Nardini, you Sista are a true rock star in my life. The level of all that has transpired since we met and became great friends and partners in education and fierceness has been one of the most incredible gifts to me—a ridiculous amount of love, respect, and gratitude to you. Laura Foster, we truly are cut from the same cloth, girlfriend. I don't even know where to begin with how grateful I am for our amazing friendship and accountability to each other. You have been such an awesome mentor to me in my life, my business, and this book. The SHIFT we have created this year excites me beyond words, and I cannot wait to see where this journey leads us.

Natasha Turner, we do not know each other very well and you may not remember many of our conversations back at The Kingsmill Club, but you have taught me much and given the world such a gift in your book, *The Hormone Diet*. I cannot thank you enough. I'm also extremely appreciative to you for allowing me to use The Hormonal Health Profile[1] from your book.

Jack Doak, you may be shocked to see your name here as it has been many years since we worked together, but my experiences working for and with you, and watching you build businesses were at times more valuable lessons than formal business classes. Your extra time and advice have not gone unnoticed and definitely not without gratitude, thank you.

Simplicity staff and members, you have all become my family these past two years; I mean that from the bottom of my heart. You have added such depth and richness to my life, and have been the fuel to my spirit for creating Simplicity and watching this truly unique, amazing space and energy continually transform. You have no idea how much joy you bring into every day when I step onto the mat and look back at all of you. You should be proud of yourselves as you have all served to be a teacher to your "teach". You are simply the best and I love you all. xo.

To my Publisher, Sheri Andrunyk, and your entire team, words can't begin to express how appreciative I was and am for all your patience and expertise along this journey.

And to you, the reader, thank you so much for taking the time to read my book. This is truly my passion, my soul, and my life. I do everything with you in mind. I look forward to bringing you more in the way of books, e-books, videos, webinars, seminars, recipes, workshops and wellness-based products, from my world to yours.

To the highest level of potential in you, Namaste,

Jenn

MY JOURNEY

As far back as I can remember, exercise has been part of my life. When I was little I taught myself how to swim, do front and back walkovers, round-offs, and handsprings in my backyard; I used to lead classes in the neighbourhood when I was five. By the age of nine, I was a member of the local gym's Cardio Kids program and an avid participant in the 20 Minute Workout program on TV. By the time I was in high school, I was heading to the gym at 6:30 a.m. with my Dad before school, setting my alarm to do the Reebok Caribbean Workout on TSN, or Breathing Space Yoga with Diane Bruni. The seed had been planted.

When I was thirteen, I won a modelling course after taking part in a contest at the local mall. Within a few years I was building my portfolio, doing professional shoots, and then at sixteen, my big moment came: I won the prestigious Top Female Model of the Year 1996 Age 16+ award at the Modelling Association of Canada (MAOC) convention and was scouted by twenty-eight agencies. I decided to sign with Ford Modelling Agency as my Toronto-based agency and my "Mother" agency became Flare Modelling Agency for international modelling. I am 5'9½" and during this period of time weighed about 125 pounds (nine less than I weigh now), and I was told to lose weight and inches off my hips at nearly every casting call I went to!

xxii The Simplicity Project

Exercise became an even bigger part of my life then, as did nutrition, in an attempt to drop the inches and make it *big* in the industry. I can honestly say I never once starved myself or contemplated anything drastic; instead I read everything I could get my hands on about nutrition and exercise. I looked forward and never looked back. I finished high school and started travelling for modelling: Miami, New York, Montréal and Japan. And, yes, was repeatedly told to lose weight. When I lived in Japan, I remember one day being out on casting calls, and the staff taking our money away from us because some of us were gaining weight and they did not want us to have the choice of what to buy and eat. Instead they gave us water and gum for what turned out to be a ten-hour day of casting calls!

That was the final straw for me! I called my agent at home, who still remains a friend to this day, and said, "Get me outta here. I am DONE!"

What I didn't recognize then that I do now is that this was one of the shaping moments in my life, and I had the option to either stifle what my gut was telling me or listen to it and make a different choice. That decision has since led to wonderful *direct* bookings with clients, and no one ever treating me that way again.

Many years after graduating from The Canadian School of Natural Nutrition in Richmond Hill and Cambrian College in Sudbury, with honours in Fitness Leisure and Health Sciences and a minor in Business Management, I decided to head back to school for a degree designation as a Registered Holistic Nutritionist. A true love affair and passion with helping people fuel their minds and feed their souls with positive, useful information was born.

Throughout all my years of exercise I had flirted with yoga here and there, but never found a class or had an experience that made me want to fully commit or move away from all my hard-core spinning, running and heavy weightlifting ... that is until one day in 2003. That day, I walked into the studio, laid out my mat and in walked this energetic, eclectic, and mesmerizing new instructor. For the next hour, Theresa moved me in ways, both mentally and physically, that I had never felt before and I LOVED it! However, when it came time for the relaxation posture, savasana, I rolled up my mat, put my shoes on, and walked out. I felt I didn't have time to lie around! One day, as I was about to head out the door, Theresa looked straight at me and kindly said, "I'm sorry Jenn, but you're going to have to unroll your mat and lay back down for savasana. It's part of the class and this class isn't over." Are you friggin' kidding me? I was not impressed! I lay back down in front of two dozen people, who were also my students and personal training clients in this gym, and I was fuming. I could not believe she just did that to me in front of everyone!

It was the best lesson and aha moment I've ever had. Theresa woke something within me, and from that day forward I made yoga classes with her part of my schedule, booking soul appointments with myself five times a week. I even went to her home where she led small classes out of her living room; you walked in, dropped ten dollars into a basket, for which you got a bottle of water and one of six places, and then proceeded to sweat and twist in close proximity to the other participants. It was AWESOME!

Seven years later, in June 2010, after many years of hard work in the industry, I decided to take the leap and open my own studio. Things moved quickly. I opened my doors on Tuesday, September 29th of the same year.

A moment of alchemy I will never forget.

From my seed-planting moment at fourteen years old to

now, I offer you the power and ability to access your deepest core potential and Simply Rock It Out!

Love Jenn

MY MESSAGE

Welcome ... You've Been Waiting!

The Simplicity Project is designed to fuel your life and transform your body from the inside out.

When you begin this food journey, don't think of it as dieting or being on a diet. Diets are temporary vehicles on the road to looking a certain way, being a certain weight or size, and measuring up to society's image of health and beauty. Diets are mainly based on calorie counting, strict portion control, deprivation, self-deprecation and are, for most people, extremely unsuccessful and painfully boring.

Instead, consider this eating plan as part of your self-renewal and self-discovery. I want you to become more educated and empowered by your food choices, to know a whole food from one that's not, to know how to combine your foods for proper nourishment and balance, to know what to shop for and what to avoid, and to know how to make the most delicious healthy meals and snacks right at home.

Ultimately, I want you to rediscover your relationship with food so that you can sit at the table, smell, chew, savour, and enjoy your food without worrying about how it will impact your weight.

It may take some getting used to (especially if you've been

feeding your body processed, fast foods and sugar-filled drinks), but you'll soon appreciate and look forward to your new way of eating. You'll be preparing and enjoying fresh, real, nutrient-dense meals. You will stop feeling like you need over-the-counter antacids or a nap after you eat, and you'll start feeling energized and transformed by your meals.

Your cravings for high-fat, sugary foods will stop and, on the days that you do indulge, your body will provide feedback instantly, motivating you to keep on your "clean eating" path.

Your commitment to your food plan is just as important to your core transformation as the Simplicity workouts. If you only commit partially you will only see AND feel partial results. Movement and food go hand in hand.

If you stick to my suggestions you will see amazing results —inside and out. After reading *The Simplicity Project* and beginning your NEW YOU journey, you will have begun to learn how food can empower you instead of taking you down. You will have a much healthier relationship with food and you will find yourself making better choices about what you let pass your lips!

High five to a new you and a lifetime of healthy, lip-smacking meals.

Much love and Namaste,

Jenn

INTRODUCTION

Over the past decade, I've developed and fine-tuned *The Simplicity Project*. This is a plan focused on practical principles that have worked phenomenally well for my clients, based on simplicity and whole foods. It is one that I truly believe will have you feeling more in touch with your body, more in tune with your energy, and ultimately leave your body better supported and nourished than ever before.

This is not a diet book, or a quick-fix geared towards rapid weight loss, or a temporary solution.

I want you to look at *The Simplicity Project* like a form of school. Your butt's back in class and the subject is YOU, baby!

That's right, welcome to the class of year RIGHT NOW, working towards your PhD in You & Your Body 101!

I will give you all the tips and tools necessary to shift today and change tomorrow. One step at a time, you will feel your world and your body changing for the better. No gimmicks. This book is the "real deal" and is the first step on your path to a more vitally simplistic way of living.

The hard truth about being healthier, stronger, feeling invigorated, and achieving a desirable body weight, is that things are not as difficult as we all make them out to be.

If we just relaxed into eating and let our intuition and appetite regulate what we ate, chose the obvious healthier options at the store or restaurant, only chewed what we needed, and worked with our bodies to move and groove, we would not have as unhealthy a society as we do today.

We are trained to run to our family doctor for every issue we have going on in our bodies. The problem here is that too often the benchmarks within the "normal" medical range are far too high and leave us being dismissed as "fine". For example: TSH levels (your thyroid stimulating hormone) in the traditional medical industry is considered normal if it is between .35 and 4.7.[2] In the holistic industry we strive to detect issues when they are beginning to brew. A reading above 2.0 is considered to be sub-optimal[3]; an early indicator that if you don't begin to make some serious lifestyle changes, you could be facing medication and a lifelong struggle with your body's internal thermostat.

We are, however, much less likely to go to our family doctor for the less serious issues like fatigue, headaches, dizziness, mood swings, or weight gain—all early signs that something is going on.

We are going to work together to eliminate the impossible battle you place upon yourself with your hormones, your cravings, and your body. My hope is that this book will help you to realize symptoms before they become ailments, and to encourage you to think and react differently about your health and well-being.

As with everything I do, I try to maintain an open mind and admit that thoughts and views in this book may change with time.

However, I do feel the core concepts and methods described in this book will stay consistent and provide a realistic template for nourishing your body and your life!

CHAPTER 1

IGNITE THE FIRE WITHIN

1.1 Your New Formula For Taking Your Health Back & Losing Weight

When you take the time to notice what is around you, the people and the energy, what you will find are some major and saddening disconnects. Many are disconnected from their bodies and how they are feeling, with no remorse or pleasure from what they are eating or where their meals are coming from. They're constantly suffering from inflammation, illness, depression and living with an overall sense of "I just need to get through the day," instead of truly LIVING the day and feeling joy in the process.

You may even find you look at yourself and notice that you too are among those living disconnected. And you can hear that little voice inside asking, "How did this happen? How did I let myself get to this point? What have I done?"

STOP THIS CONVERSATION RIGHT NOW!

Move from your past: your past choices of poor food, lack of movement and lack of care and respect for your body and MOVE FORWARD!

Don't waste another second in the land of over-analyzing and under-valuing your time. You have defined that you don't feel well and that you would like to feel better... CONGRATULATIONS! Now what?

CHANGE. It takes one simple change to create a SHIFT.

If there was only one choice for you to make that would hold the most weight, the most impact on your health and well-being, it would be the food you are purchasing, preparing and consuming. Everything that enters your mouth, whether it is the food you chew or beverages you drink, has a direct impact on your body, mind, and spirit. I learned this quite literally when I began changing the way I ate and felt about food more than seventeen years ago. Not only did my body begin to change, but I felt happier and more connected to myself. Something shifted in me that I never expected or even thought to look for. But there it was. Changing the way I ate, the way I perceived food and nourishment for my body, changed my life and who I was completely ... it led me on the path to where I am today.

And now today is your day.

Your first task: Create a reasonable, yet challenging and meaningful goal for yourself with regard to your new way of eating. It can be as simple as no more eating right before bed or in bed, or drinking two litres of water a day, to something more aggressive like giving up wheat. Everyone is at a different level of "done with feeling like crap" and everyone has different goals. You decide what is most important to you, what you are up for and most importantly, WHAT YOU CAN HANDLE.

But ... in order for this shift of consciousness to be impactful enough, you are going to have to push yourself beyond your comfort zone. Being uncomfortable is a good thing here; it means things are changing for the better.

I, _____ (your name), am going to begin

_____

_____

_____

How I would describe myself now _____

_____

_____

In order to be successful with my goal of _____

_____,

I will need to _____

_____

_____

Some things that might get in my way _____

_____

_____

_____

How I plan to get out of my own way _____

_____

_____

Why I am worth this journey and how I will describe myself once

I am done _____

_____

_____

Be The Change You Want To FEEL ...

When it comes to nutrition, dieting, shopping, cooking, and eating a well-balanced diet, there is no such thing as black and white. The food and nutrition industry is grey and suffocating in thousands upon thousands of books, programs, and gurus claiming to be THE voice for you. The reality is that you need to be patient, you need to spend time moving through the information that is available to you and, more importantly, while reading and digesting ... LISTEN to your inner guide and guru. What resonates most with you in terms of the information? What do you think you could begin to do right now that wouldn't be overwhelmingly life-altering and excruciating; something you could do a little planning for today and start tomorrow?

This is where I would recommend you begin ... at the beginning.

We tend to put these huge expectations and parameters upon ourselves that almost immediately set us up for disaster. This time, choose to slow down and learn something along the way.

Too many believe that we can get healthy if we lose weight. The reality is that we must be healthy to lose weight. When you complete your Hormonal Health Profile, you will begin to see exactly what has been going on all these years, and finally begin to optimize your health and hormonal balance, lose fat, and restore your health and vitality.

The Simplicity Project is really a "Living More Simply" program, which includes understanding the causes of why you feel less than optimal, and a holistic wellness approach for shifting you out of it.

Get Your Engines Ready!!!

1.2 The Stress & Imbalance Of Today's Metabolic System

One of the primary factors determining your body weight is metabolism, the internal furnace that regulates fat burning. Everyone's metabolism is different, which is why some people seem to be able to eat anything and remain lean while others can pack on the pounds so easily.

Having a healthy digestive system is the essential foundation to having a strong metabolism. The old saying is, "You are what you eat"; I say, "You are what you absorb and what you fail to eliminate (poop)!"

Many of us are suffering from major internal inflammation hindering our ability to ever lose weight or feel great. Most people have one of two digestive scenarios unfolding. The first is an under-active digestive system which is characterized by bloating, gas, belching, headaches, low blood sugar, acne, constipation, feeling full for a long time after eating, and the need for a snooze after meals. Typically, these individuals also crave caffeine, sodas, chocolate, candy, and cookies and must hit the 1:00 p.m. sweet zone before they become a complete bitch on wheels. Within a couple of hours, they hit the 3:00 p.m. nap zone and the vicious cycle begins again.

The other individuals are suffering from an over-active stomach with excess acidity, burning, sourness in the stomach, reflux, heartburn, frequent and often explosive or loose bowel movements, and craving a lot of stimulants like coffee, cigarettes, and alcohol. These people tend to crave more salty, savoury foods than sweet, and usually approach their meals with the "open, chew twice, and swallow" technique that is contributing to the raging fire happening in their bellies and eventually their butts!

Seventy percent of our immune system lies within our digestive tract. Compromises to our digestion such as allergies, sensitivities, over-consumption, parasites, yeast overgrowth, and stress negatively affect not only our digestion but also our overall immunity. I begin the treatment of all my clients with focusing on optimizing and healing their digestion. I truly believe that to get out of your rut, you've got to start with your gut!

1.3 **You Will Not Count Calories**

I hope you are starting to understand why typical weight loss diets don't work. We all know the old routine: it's Sunday and after feeling totally gross from the weekend, the week, the month, the year, whatever, we make the solemn oath that, "That's It! Starting tomorrow (Monday) I am going on a diet!" Meanwhile, we still have all the food vices in our cupboards and fridges and have done no work to prepare the foundation of this "plan".

Monday morning we wake, have some oatmeal and fruit and give ourselves a pat on the back. We have a piece of fruit for a mid-morning snack and salad for lunch ... Yes! High five to me! Now it's 1:30 p.m. and the plan starts to fall apart. You're searching for something, anything to conquer your craving. And there it is, the vending machine. You charge it like you are suddenly part of the defence line for the Chicago Bears (my hubby's team) and you press C4, the chocolate bar ... VICTORY!

This victory is short lived by the crashing hit you get from team "blood sugar dropping". You now feel horrible and guilty, and convince yourself that you have totally blown it and might as well just throw in the towel. Sound familiar?

Life is going to happen; sweet, yummy, not-so-good-for-us food is going to happen. So here is my advice: lick your lips and enjoy it. Seriously, what are you going to do about it now? Go in after it? Guess what the best part is? You didn't blow your new way of eating. That's right, because you have another meal coming up in a few hours and you get to choose all over again—this time just a little healthier.

You Can't Excessively Restrict or Count Your Calories as Your Weight Loss Approach

When you do, this happens:

- You feel hungrier because the body responds to calorie restriction by releasing hormones that increase your appetite.
- Your level of thyroid hormone drops, causing a slow-down in your metabolism.

- Your level of the stress hormone, cortisol, increases in response to the physical stress of skipping meals or insufficient carbohydrate intake.

- Reproductive function slows because your sex hormones change due to insufficient intake, contributing to excessive PMS, menstrual changes, etc.

When your hormones get thrown out of whack, your tendency to overeat and overindulge kicks in. Then your body starts to suffer through highs and lows of up and down calorie intake. Your body is very intelligent. As a defence, if you do not feed it well or often enough, it will learn, *from you*, to hold on to any new food coming in as fat, just in case you don't eat for a while again or you don't eat what the body needs. Diet food products do this continuously. The end result is havoc on your system, more weight gain, cravings, depression, mood swings, no energy, and worst of all, a damaged metabolism and the loss of precious, metabolically active muscle tissue.

Cheers to Whole Foods!

Here's the beauty part though: when you choose fresh (organic when possible) fruits and vegetables, healthy lean sources of protein like organic meat, chicken, fish, and eggs, good quality essential fatty acids, raw nuts and seeds, lots of water, and properly balanced snacks and meals, your body will finally get what it needs and release its grip on you. When you eat only nutrient-dense food, you won't be able to over-eat and have crazy portions—you will be too full of the good stuff! Plus, your digestion will be enhanced and your body will break-down food more effectively, meaning you will absorb more of it.

I have been eating this way for over ten years now and have stayed within my current weight by five pounds through two pregnancies, a lot of celebrations, some down days, and the stress of starting a new business. I don't punish myself with feelings of wishing I hadn't eaten certain things; I choose every bite that goes into my mouth and I OWN that. I never say I can't or I'm not allowed; instead I say, "I choose to eat this" or, "I choose not to." Just as you do when you grocery shop, you vote for health and well-being each time you eat.

What will your next vote be?

1.4 Your Weight Loss Friends & Your Weight Loss Foes

Losing weight is more than simply burning more calories than you consume or just eating less in the first place. There is a myriad of events that must take place in order to shed the extra weight you are carrying. First of all, your body needs to produce certain hormones. Secondly, your body and brain must be able to receive the messages these hormones are trying to send. Otherwise, you will never feel full, satisfied, or know when to put the fork down!

No hormone in your entire body works on its own. Each one interacts and influences each other, which is why, when there is a spike in one hormone, another one usually drops. Too much or too little of ANY hormone in the body can cause major disturbances, and will interfere not only with your metabolism, but also your sleep, sex drive, energy, and over-all wellness.

The top four hormones that affect your metabolism are insulin, cortisol, estrogen and ghrelin.

Too Much Insulin

Insulin is a hormone made by the pancreas that helps the body store and use glucose. I like to think of insulin as being the key to a car. The car is the body and instead of gas it runs on glucose. The gas gauge is like a blood glucose meter. We can run without it for a while, but it is really useful for telling us when we are going to run out of energy. Without the key to the car (insulin) we are not going anywhere. We need insulin to use the sugar to give us energy.

The food we eat is broken down into sugar (glucose). Once this happens it triggers your pancreas to release the insulin hormone. The insulin is released in relation to the amount of sugar in the bloodstream, so, the more sugar you consume, the more insulin you produce.

However, your body only has the ability to use up so much glucose at a time, and any extra is stored in the muscles or the liver as glycogen for later use. The room available for extra glucose to be stored in these areas is only so big, and what isn't stored here doesn't vanish into thin air. Your body will hold onto excess insulin and store it as fat for later use. If this is how you are eating or functioning on a daily basis, the "extra" sugar being stored in your fat becomes more than the body can either burn off or handle and you end up with major weight gain, low energy, and unbearable cravings. The not-so-awesome BONUS: this excess insulin also blocks your body's ability to use this stored fat as an energy source.

This may explain why you are holding onto a lot of extra weight around your mid-section and you feel like nothing you do helps you to lose weight and your "muffin top", which should now be called your "insulin top".

Having too much insulin will also cause you to overeat and consume more calories because: a) it blocks signals to your brain from the appetite-suppressing hormone, leptin, causing you to eat more, and b) it creates a spike in dopamine, your feel-good, pleasure hormone in the brain. This hormone spurs addiction and literally makes you become addicted to food!

The main ways we create excess insulin are:

- Too much CRAP! Processed, sugary, chemically created foods and drinks
- Too little protein, fat and fibre; the three key elements that, when combined with carbs, slow down the rate at which insulin enters the bloodstream and helps to maintain healthy blood-sugar levels
- Stress
- Overburdened liver and impaired digestion
- Steroid based medicines, antibiotics, birth control pills, synthetic hormones
- Lack of exercise or too much exercise (yes, you can exercise too much!)

Beyond making us fat-storing machines, insulin can also give us symptoms and feelings such as: heart palpitations, fatigue and mood swings, sweating, anxiety, insomnia and poor concentration, acne, abnormal hair growth, and shrinking, sagging breasts. In men, the more insulin they have tends to convert their testosterone into estrogen and create man-boobs, big bellies and can lead to erectile dysfunction.

AB Fat Central a.k.a. Cortisol!

Cortisol is the "awesome", fat-packing stress hormone that is produced by your adrenals (two glands that sit on top of your kidneys and also produce adrenaline). Your adrenals are quite literally like your body's internal SWAT team in response to stress. This ability to respond quickly to stressful situations is both impressive and essential, however, it's highly over stimulated and misused by many of us on a daily basis.

The immediate production of stress hormones are designed by the body to be in response to something sudden, immediate, and life-threatening. Think about the old story of a bear coming out of the forest in front of you and you suddenly have this surge of energy (adrenaline) that helps you hightail it out of there. The good thing about short-term stress like that is, it happens; you deal with it and then move on.

The problematic stress is the everyday "bear" chasing us down: raising children, finances, work or relationship-related stress, poor diet, no exercise or exercising like a freakin' mad person wearing a tiara that says Cardio Queen, feeling overwhelmed, and in poor health. This type of chronic stress— whether real or imagined—causes your body to release high amounts of the stress hormone, cortisol.

Unlike adrenalin, which draws from your fat stores for energy during stress, cortisol consumes your muscle tissue for fuel. Chronic stress will lead to muscle wasting and higher blood sugar levels, simply because your body is struggling to figure out a way to adapt.

Some of the other symptoms and effects of excess cortisol are:

- Decreased metabolic rate
- Blood sugar imbalances
- Thyroid dysfunction
- Decreased serotonin, the happy hormone, causing depression and increased carb cravings
- Insomnia and low libido

The most common characteristics of cortisol imbalance that I see in clients are extreme difficulty getting out of bed in the morning, excess fatigue throughout the day, and an over-stimulated hamster wheel at night that makes it difficult to calm the body down enough to fall asleep—a "wired but tired" feeling.

The key to achieving optimal health and a strong, lean body is learning to implement the strategies throughout this book in order to control your cortisol production. Managing cortisol is truly the key to decreased stress in your body and overall wellness!

Excess Estrogen or Estrogen Dominance

Estrogen dominance is, I believe, the cause of many hormonal imbalances we see today. It describes a condition where a woman can have deficient, normal, or excessive estrogen, but has little or no progesterone to balance its effects in the body. Even a woman with low estrogen levels can have estrogen dominance symptoms if she doesn't have any progesterone.

Estrogen Dominance Symptoms:

- Acceleration of the aging process
- Allergies, including asthma, hives, rashes, sinus congestion
- Autoimmune disorders such as lupus and hypoactive thyroid
- Breast cancer (estrogen feeds many cancers)
- Breast tenderness
- Cervical dysplasia

- Cold hands and feet as a symptom of thyroid dysfunction
- Decreased sex drive
- Depression with anxiety or agitation
- Dry eyes
- Early onset of menstruation
- Endometrial (uterine) cancer
- Fat gain, especially around the abdomen, hips and thighs
- Fatigue
- Fibrocystic breasts
- Foggy thinking
- Gallbladder disease
- Hair loss
- Headaches
- Hypoglycemia
- Increased blood clotting (increasing risk of strokes)
- Infertility
- Irregular menstrual periods
- Irritability
- Insomnia
- Magnesium deficiency
- Memory loss
- Mood swings
- Osteoporosis
- Polycystic ovaries
- Premenopausal bone loss

- PMS
- Prostate cancer
- Sluggish metabolism
- Thyroid dysfunction mimicking hypothyroidism
- Uterine cancer
- Uterine fibroids
- Water retention, bloating
- Zinc deficiency

Why & How Has Estrogen Dominance Become Such an Issue?

There are only two ways extra estrogen builds up in our bodies: you are either producing too much, or it is coming in via your environment or food choices. You would have to virtually live in a bubble to escape the excess estrogen we're exposed to through pesticides, plastics, industrial waste products, car exhaust, meat, soaps, and much of the carpeting, furniture, and panelling that we live with indoors every day. You may have on-and-off sinus problems, headaches, dry eyes, asthma, or cold hands and feet for example, and not know to attribute them to your exposure to xenoestrogens (chemical forms of the hormone estrogen).

Women are far more susceptible to estrogen dominance (although the rate is rising with men) because of how many bodily products we use: make-up, lotions, creams, perfumes, even your feminine hygiene products. Unless they are organic, they contain chemical forms (xenoestrogen) of estrogen that burden your system with too much.

Too Little Estrogen Can Also Create Problems ...

Estrogen helps your cells to effectively respond to insulin so when estrogen levels drop, insulin levels tend to increase. This is most common in peri-menopause and menopause. Making matters even worse is that during this time there is also a drop in the happy hormone, serotonin, which drives us to crave more sweets, treats, and carbs ... and yet again produce even more insulin! Are you beginning to see a pattern?

Great Ghrelin!

You know when you and everyone else around you hears your stomach growl? That is the sound of your stomach producing ghrelin. Ghrelin is the hunger hormone. It's made in the stomach, and it tells the brain when it's time to eat. The problem with ghrelin is that when we eat nutrient-devoid foods and not enough healthy calories, ghrelin production can increase, making us feel hungrier, and may cause us to eat more than we really need. Eating healthier foods and ensuring that you are not going beyond three to four hours without eating will help to keep the hunger-hormone, ghrelin, in check.

Your Weight Loss Friends

We will delve much deeper into each of these in Chapter 3, but I will give you a quick preview of the specifics. In order to effectively lose weight AND keep it off, there are a few areas of the body that need to be in proper balance:

- Your thyroid
- Your adrenals

- DHEA (Dehydroepiandrosterone) and your growth hormone
- Leptin
- Your sleep must be adequate
- Your exercise must be in alignment with your goals, the reality of your pace in life, and what your body may NOT be craving

Now let's move on to your Simplicity Hormonal Health Profile in the following section.

1.5 How Balanced Are You?
Complete Your Hormonal Health Profile

Thank you to one of my most profound teachers, Dr. Natasha Turner, author of the best-selling book, *The Hormone Diet*, for use of this profiling system.

Inflammation: (please check all that apply)

- [ ] Sagging, thinning or wrinkling skin
- [x] Spider veins
- [ ] Cellulite
- [x] Eczema, rashes, acne
- [x] PMS
- [x] Fibrocystic breast
- [ ] Menopause (women)
- [ ] Heart disease
- [ ] Fatigue
- [ ] High cholesterol and high blood pressure

- ☐ Low to no exercise
- ☐ Aches and pains
- ☐ Water retention in hands and feet
- ☐ Gout
- ☐ Alzheimer's disease and/or Parkinson's disease
- ☑ Depression
- ☐ Fibromyalgia
- ☐ Increased pain or poor pain tolerance
- ☑ Headaches or migraines
- ☐ High alcohol consumption
- ☐ Allergies
- ☐ Autoimmune disease
- ☐ Fat gain around abdomen
- ☐ Loss of bone density
- ☐ Type 2 diabetes
- ☐ Sleep disruptions
- ☐ Irritable Bowel Syndrome (IBS)
- ☐ Gas and bloating
- ☑ Constipation, diarrhoea or nausea

TOTAL (Warning Score: > 12)

Excess Insulin/Insulin Resistance: (please check all that apply)

- ☐ Sagging, thinning or wrinkling skin
- ☑ Cellulite
- ☐ Infertility
- ☐ Irregular cycles

- [ ] Polycystic Ovarian Syndrome (PCOS)
- [ ] Abnormal hair growth
- [ ] Vision changes
- [ ] Menopause
- [ ] Heart disease
- [x] Fatigue
- [ ] Insomnia
- [ ] High cholesterol/blood pressure
- [ ] Lack of exercise
- [ ] Burning feet in bed
- [x] Poor memory and concentration
- [ ] No or low sex drive
- [ ] Fat gain around mid-section and upper arms/ puffy face
- [x] Hypoglycemia/low blood sugar
- [x] Tired after eating
- [ ] Type 2 diabetes

TOTAL (Warning Score: >10)

Low Dopamine: (please check all that apply)

- [x] Fatigue, especially in the morning
- [ ] Lack of exercise
- [ ] Restless leg syndrome
- [x] Poor memory
- [ ] Parkinson's disease
- [x] Depression
- [ ] Loss of libido

☐ Addictive eating or binge eating

☐ Weight gain/obesity

☑ Cravings for sweets, carbs, junk food or fast food

TOTAL (Warning Score: > 4)

Low Serotonin: (please check all that apply)

☑ PMS characterized by hypoglycemia, sugar cravings, sweet cravings

☑ Depression

☑ Fatigue

☐ Feeling wired at night

☐ Lack of sweating

☑ Poor memory

☐ Loss of libido

☑ Depression, anxiety, irritability or seasonal affective disorder (SAD)

☑ Loss of motivation or competitive edge

☑ Low self-esteem

☑ Inability to make decisions

☐ Obsessive-compulsive disorder

☐ Bulimia or binge eating

☐ Fibromyalgia

☐ Increased pain or poor pain tolerance

☑ Headaches or migraines

☐ High alcohol consumption

☐ Generalized overweight/weight gain/obesity

☑ Cravings for sweets or carbohydrates

☐ Constant hunger or increased appetite

☐ Failure to sleep in total darkness

☐ Inability to sleep in, no matter how late going to bed

☑ Less than seven and a half hours of sleep per night

☐ Irritable bowel

☐ Constipation

☐ Nausea

☑ Use of corticosteroids

TOTAL (Warning Score: > 8)

Excess Cortisol: (please check all that apply)

☐ Wrinkling, thinning or skin has lost its fullness

☑ Acne

☐ Hair loss

☑ PMS

☑ Infertility or absent menses (unrelated to menopause)

☐ Feeling wired at night

☐ High cholesterol or blood pressure

☐ Lack of exercise

☐ Heart palpitations

☐ Loss of muscle tone in arms and legs

☑ Cold hands and feet

☐ Water retention in face/puffiness

☑ Poor memory or concentration

☐ Loss of libido

☑ Depression, anxiety, irritability or seasonal affective disorder

- ☑ Low self-esteem
- ☐ High alcohol consumption
- ☐ Frequent colds and flus
- ☑ Hives, bronchitis, allergies (food or environmental), asthma or autoimmune disease
- ☐ Fat gain around "love handles" or abdomen
- ☐ A "buffalo lump" of fat on neck or upper back
- ☐ Difficulty building or maintaining muscle
- ☐ Loss of bone density or osteoporosis
- ☑ Cravings for sweets or carbs, hypoglycemia or constant hunger
- ☐ Difficulty falling asleep
- ☐ Failure to sleep in total darkness
- ☐ Difficulty staying asleep (especially waking between 2:00 a.m. and 4:00 a.m.)
- ☑ Less than seven and a half hours of sleep per night
- ☐ IBS (Irritable bowel syndrome) or frequent gas and bloating
- ☑ Use of corticosteroids

TOTAL (Warning score: > 10)

Low DHEA (Dehydroepiandrosterone: (please check all that apply)
- ☐ Dry skin
- ☐ Heart disease
- ☐ Erectile dysfunction
- ☐ Andropause
- ☑ Fatigue

- [ ] Feeling wired at night
- [ ] Poor tolerance for exercise
- [ ] Lack of exercise
- [ ] Loss of muscle tone in arms and legs
- [ ] Poor memory or concentration
- [ ] Irritability or easily agitated
- [ ] Loss of libido
- [ ] Depression
- [ ] Loss of motivation or competitive edge
- [ ] Autoimmune disease
- [ ] Fat gain around "love handles"
- [ ] Fat gain over the triceps
- [ ] Fat gain around abdomen
- [ ] Difficulty building or maintaining muscle
- [ ] Difficulty staying asleep (especially waking between 2:00 a.m. and 4:00 a.m.)
- [ ] Use of corticosteroids

TOTAL (Warning score: > 7)

Excess Estrogen: (please check all that apply)

- [ ] Spider veins
- [ ] Varicose veins
- [ ] Cellulite
- [ ] Heavy menstrual bleeding
- [ ] PMS characterized by breast tenderness, water retention, bloating, swelling and/or weight gain
- [ ] Fibrocystic breast disease

- [ ] Prostate enlargement
- [ ] Erectile dysfunction
- [ ] Breast growth (men)
- [ ] Loss of morning erection
- [x] Irritability, mood swings or anxiety
- [x] Headaches or migraines
- [ ] High alcohol consumption (>4 drinks per week for women and >7 drinks per week for men)
- [x] Autoimmune disease or allergies
- [ ] Fat gain around "love handles" or abdomen (men)
- [ ] Fat gain at the hips (women)
- [ ] Current use of hormone replacement therapy or birth control pills

TOTAL (Warning score: >6)

Low Estrogen: (please check all that apply)

- [ ] Dry or sagging skin
- [ ] Thinning skin or skin has lost its fullness
- [ ] Hair loss
- [ ] Dry eyes or cataracts (women)
- [x] PMS characterized by depression, hypoglycemia, sugar cravings and/or sweet cravings
- [x] Infertility or absent menses (not related to menopause)
- [ ] Painful intercourse and/or vaginal dryness
- [ ] Shrinking or sagging breasts
- [ ] Urinary incontinence (stress or otherwise)
- [ ] Menopause

- ☑ Fatigue
- ☐ Hot flashes
- ☐ High cholesterol or blood pressure
- ☑ Poor memory or concentration
- ☑ Irritability
- ☐ Loss of libido
- ☑ Depression or mood swings
- ☑ Headaches or migraines
- ☐ Fat gain around "love handles" or abdomen (menopausal women)
- ☐ Loss of bone density or osteoporosis
- ☑ Cravings for sweets or carbohydrates
- ☐ Difficulty falling or staying asleep

TOTAL (Warning score: > 8)

Excess Progesterone: (please check all that apply)

- ☑ Acne
- ☐ PMS characterized by depression
- ☑ Infertility
- ☐ Water retention
- ☑ Depression
- ☑ Headaches or migraines
- ☐ Frequent colds and flus
- ☐ Weight gain or difficulty losing weight
- ☐ Current use of hormone replacement therapy or birth control pills

TOTAL (Warning score: > 4)

Low Progesterone: (please check all that apply)

- [ ] Dry skin or skin that has lost its fullness
- [x] Spider or varicose veins
- [ ] Hair loss
- [ ] Short menstrual cycle (< 28 days)
- [x] PMS characterized by breast tenderness, anxiety, sleep disruptions, headaches, menstrual spotting, water retention, bloating and/or weight gain
- [x] Infertility or absent menses (not related to menopause)
- [ ] Fibrocystic breast disease
- [ ] Menopause (women); andropause (men)
- [ ] Prostate enlargement
- [ ] Hot flashes
- [ ] Lack of sweating
- [x] Feeling cold or cold hands/feet
- [ ] Heart palpitations
- [ ] Water retention
- [x] Irritability and/or anxiety
- [ ] Loss of libido
- [x] Headaches or migraines
- [ ] Autoimmune disease, hives, asthma or allergies
- [ ] Loss of bone density or osteoporosis
- [ ] Difficulty falling or staying asleep

TOTAL (Warning score: > 6)

Excess Testosterone: (please check all that apply)

- [ ] Dry skin
- [ ] Thinning skin or skin has lost its fullness
- [ ] Painful intercourse
- [ ] Heart disease (men)
- [ ] Erectile dysfunction
- [ ] Andropause (men)
- [ ] Loss of morning erection
- [x] Fatigue
- [ ] Poor tolerance for exercise
- [ ] Lack of exercise
- [ ] Heart palpitations
- [ ] Loss of muscle tone in arms and legs
- [x] Poor memory or concentration
- [ ] Loss of libido
- [x] Depression or anxiety
- [x] Loss of motivation or competitive edge
- [x] Low self-esteem
- [x] Difficulty making decisions
- [ ] Headaches or migraines (men)
- [ ] Gaining fat around abdomen or "love handles" (men and women)
- [ ] Difficulty building or maintaining muscle
- [ ] Loss of bone density or osteoporosis (men and women)
- [ ] Sleep apnea (men)
- [x] Use of corticosteroids

TOTAL (Warning score: >8)

High Testosterone: (please check all that apply)

- ☑ Acne
- ☐ Hair loss (scalp)
- ☐ Abnormal hair growth on face (women)
- ☑ Infertility
- ☐ Shrinking or sagging breasts
- ☐ Prostate enlargement
- ☐ Irritability, aggression or easily agitated
- ☑ Headaches or migraines (women)
- ☐ Fat gain at abdomen (women)
- ☐ Generalized overweight/weight gain/obesity (women)
- ☐ Cravings for sweets or carbohydrates (women)
- ☐ Constant hunger or increased appetite (women)
- ☐ Fatty liver (women)

TOTAL (Warning score: > 5)

Low Thyroid: (please check all that apply)

- ☐ Dry skin and/or hair
- ☑ Acne
- ☐ Hair loss
- ☐ Brittle hair and/or nails
- ☐ PMS, infertility, long menstrual cycle (> 30 days) or irregular periods
- ☐ Fibrocystic breast disease
- ☐ Abnormal lactation
- ☐ Fatigue
- ☑ Lack of sweating, feeling cold or cold hands and feet
- ☐ High cholesterol

- ☐ Poor tolerance for exercise
- ☐ Heart palpitations
- ☐ Outer edge of eyebrows thinning
- ☐ Aches and pains
- ☐ Water retention/puffiness in hands or feet
- ☑ Poor memory
- ☐ Loss of libido
- ☑ Depression
- ☐ Loss of motivation or competitive edge
- ☐ Iron deficiency anemia
- ☐ Hives
- ☐ Generalized overnight/weight gain/obesity
- ☐ Constipation
- ☑ Use of corticosteroids
- ☐ Current use of synthetic hormone replacement therapy or birth control pills

TOTAL (Warning score: > 8)

Low Melatonin: (please check all that apply)

- ☐ Andropause (men); menopause (women)
- ☑ Fatigue
- ☑ Night eating syndrome
- ☐ High alcohol consumption
- ☐ Frequent colds and flus
- ☐ Cravings for sweets or carbohydrates; increased appetite
- ☐ Difficulty falling asleep
- ☐ Failing to sleep in total darkness

- [ ] Difficulty staying asleep (especially between 2:00 a.m. and 4:00 a.m.)
- [ ] Sleep apnea
- [ ] Less than seven and a half hours of sleep per night
- [ ] Use of corticosteroids

TOTAL (Warning score: >4)

Low Growth Hormone: (please check all that apply)

- [ ] Dry skin
- [ ] Thinning skin or skin has lost its fullness
- [ ] Sagging skin
- [ ] Menopause (women); andropause (men)
- [ ] Fatigue
- [ ] Poor tolerance for exercise
- [ ] Lack of exercise
- [ ] Loss of muscle tone in arms or legs
- [ ] High alcohol consumption
- [ ] Fat gain around "love handles" or abdomen
- [ ] Difficulty building or maintaining muscle
- [ ] Loss of bone density or osteoporosis
- [ ] Generalized overweight/weight gain/obesity
- [ ] Failing to sleep in total darkness
- [ ] Difficulty staying asleep (especially waking between 2:00 a.m. and 4:00 a.m.)
- [ ] Sleep apnea
- [ ] Use of corticosteroids

TOTAL (Warning score: >6)

1.6 **What Do Your Results Mean?**

The Hormonal Health Profile is not meant to be used or looked upon like a diagnostic test. It is merely a helpful tool to open your eyes to how you are really feeling in certain areas of your body, and what your signs and symptoms could be telling you about specific systems or glands, e.g., you scored high for under-active thyroid or excess cortisol.

The problem with so many of us today is that we're always running to the doctor, the pharmacist, or the psychiatrist, to tell us what is wrong. Then, we take pills to make our symptoms stop, instead of looking in the mirror and having a conversation with ourselves about what's really going on.

The Simplicity Project is geared towards rebalancing your body, diminishing the majority of your uncomfortable symptoms, and helping you lose the extra weight that has been plaguing you for so long.

ANY steps or suggestions you choose to take or make happen from this book are going to positively impact your overall state of well-being and your life.

You are on a Simplistic path to bliss my friends … enjoy the scenery.

CHAPTER 2

TO GET OUT OF YOUR RUT, YOU'VE GOT TO START WITH YOUR GUT

2.1 Digestion & Assimilation: You Are What You Eat, And More Importantly, What You Digest!

Do You Need To Heal Your Digestion?

Are you ...

- Often bloated and embarrassingly flatulent?
- Suffering from constipation or diarrhoea?
- Allergic or sensitive to certain foods?
- Suffering from stomach aches and upset often?
- Up at night with reflux and heartburn?

- Scared to eat lunch, as you feel so tired and sluggish afterward?

- Think you've taken too many antibiotics in the past?

- From a family with a history of IBS, Chron's, Colitis, Diverticulitis or Colon Cancer?

- Just not sure what to eat anymore, as it seems most foods cause you discomfort?

You have heard the old saying a million times before: You are what you eat. I believe this statement to be even more true: You are not only what you eat, but more importantly what you digest—AND don't *poop* out!

If you're consuming foods that are processed, unhealthy, and out of balance with your body, you are creating a toxic load in your cells, tissues, organs, and colon, literally polluting yourself from the inside out.

Ideally, proper balance would go a little something like this:

You eat good food.

You fill your "tank" with optimal fuel to contribute to your health.

The rest comes out with ease and within a healthy range of time.

Unfortunately, after years of talking to clients, friends, and family about poop, this is not the case for most people. Hence why you are reading this section with eyes WIDE open and squirming slightly in your seat.

You will begin to resonate with, and understand more fully, your new healthy digestive BEING mantra:

I am what I DIGEST, and that is why
WHAT I eat is so important.

Without trying to get too science-nerdy on you, here is a little 101 on your digestive system:

2.2 Digestion 101[4]

Sight and Smell. You know when you walk past a bakery, smell fresh delicious bread being made and think to yourself, "I am drooling … that smells so good!" *Well, you probably are drooling.* The sight and smell of food is what gets the digestive juices flowing and stimulates the digestive tract. This is why it is important to look at what you are eating so that the digestive process can begin.

Mouth. Saliva contains an enzyme, amylase, which starts to break down carbohydrates in the mouth. Take the time to chew your food, and you will be on your way to solving many of your digestive ailments. The tongue in a healthy mouth is soft, pink, and wet, but if your tongue is dry, yellowed, or cracked, you could be in urgent need of a digestive overhaul. Now look in the mirror, stick out your tongue and say ahhhhhh!

Esophagus. When you swallow and your food leaves your mouth, it enters the esophagus. This long pipe connects your mouth to your stomach and is lined with a delicate mucus membrane that helps food slide down. If your stomach rejects the food, it travels back up as vomit—a mixture of acids and digestive enzymes that can damage the esophagus. Don't ignore reflux of any sort as it can lead to ulceration and even cancer.

Stomach. The stomach muscles work to churn your food, mixing it with hydrochloric acid (HCL), protective mucus, and protein-digesting enzymes, as well as special hormones that control the whole show. This process starts the breakdown of foods into smaller pieces, which the intestines can then absorb into your blood stream.

Small Intestine. Small is a crazy name for the longest part of your bowel—it is twenty-three feet long! This is where all the digestive action takes place with protein, carbs, and fats being broken down into tiny components. The absorption of these digested nutrients into the blood stream begins in the small intestines.

Large Intestine. The large intestine, five feet long, plays no actual role in digestion itself, but still holds an important role in the absorption of water and mineral salts from the stool as it passes through. It also helps remove bacteria from the bowel during each bowel movement.

Liver and Gallbladder. The liver is the primary organ of digestion as it helps the body to digest and store nutrients. For example, the liver stores vitamins, iron, and several other minerals until the body requires them, as well as storing glucose, which the body needs for energy. It also forms bile salts, which are then stored in the gallbladder until we need them to help with the digestion of fats. We will chat more about the liver in a bit!

Pancreas. The pancreas supports digestion by producing digestive enzymes that break down our food, as well as an alkaline liquid to reduce the acidity of the food after it leaves the stomach and enters the small intestine. It also produces hormones, such as insulin, that help with the metabolism of carbs.

Phew!!! Okay, well, hopefully you're not too glazed over now and you get the gist about your innards!

2.3 How Digestive Troubles Can Begin

Stress. When your body is under stress, you move into flight or fight mode. Stress can happen in many ways: financially, physically, work, home, and with your children and loved ones. Even what would appear to be a silly habit like standing while you eat can create significant stress on your digestive system. When you are standing, the blood in your body is out of your gut and into your limbs and brain to keep you standing and your muscles firing optimally. When the digestive tract has a drastically reduced blood supply, it produces fewer enzymes. So your food literally ends up hanging out in your stomach and intestines, rotting and fermenting. When not properly digested, bloating, gas, discomfort, and irritation to the lining of the bowels results. The more often this cycle happens and the longer the undigested food hangs around, the more likely it is that you will start to reabsorb some of the toxins from that food.

I believe GROSS is the word you are looking for!

Not Including Probiotics In Your Everyday. Probiotics are hugely important in your digestive health. These good bacteria enhance the breakdown and absorption of vitamins and proteins, and produce substances that help to reduce cholesterol and regulate blood sugars. They also keep in check unfriendly bacteria, which thrive in sugar, alcohol, and refined foods, and cause gas, bloating, and even conditions such as irritable bowel syndrome. Such things as antibiotics, the birth control pill, and a poor diet damage good flora. When this happens we stop absorbing nutrients properly and bad bacteria can flourish leading to problems such as IBS, Candida, and bowel disease.

Poor Hydration. Without enough water in your body daily, it will be virtually impossible for you to have regular bowel movements, detoxify your system, absorb nutrients optimally, or have any energy at all. Aim for at least two to three litres of pure, good quality water daily. Hydration rich fruits and veggies plus organic herbal teas will also help you achieve your hydration goals.

Not Enough Fibre. Fibre is essential to help decrease your appetite, your cravings, stabilize your blood sugar, add bulk to your stool and it works as an internal exfoliator to the walls of your intestines and your colon. Ensuring you get enough fibre daily, roughly 25 to 40 grams, has also been shown to reduce your risk of colon cancer.

2.4 Digestive Upset Can Lead To More Than Burps, Toots And The Scoots

If your "small" digestive issues are ignored such as excessive belching, gas, bloating, reflux etc. and you mask them with over the counter or even prescription medicines, then the lining of the bowel can become very damaged. This abuse and damage may cause you to develop a "leaky gut" in which the damaged bowel lining allows partially digested food directly into the blood stream. Your immune system sees the leaked food as an antigen (an unwanted invader), will initiate an immune response to these undigested particles, and you may ultimately develop an allergy to it. This means that each time you eat this particular food, your immune system goes on full alert to protect you and you feel tired because of the huge amount of energy directed into defending you. The weaker and more tired you are, the more chance the bad flora has to thrive—and so it goes, on and on and on.

Side-effects during digestive clean-up. There is always the chance of a healing crisis when you clear out your digestive system and your body begins to repair itself. The chances of crises increase, the longer the clear-out. You may experience a slight fever and a few aches and pains in the digestive tract. On longer digestion clean-ups, you may have a runny nose, breakouts, sore eyes, aches and pains in your joints, headaches, dry skin, and tiredness, all of which should pass quickly. Try taking a plant-based digestive enzyme, which will help to break down protein, fats, carbs, and plant fibre. They are also very useful in preventing bloating after you have eaten.

You would also be wise to add a probiotic to your regimen if you haven't already:

Genuine Health live probio + o3mega: two capsules upon rising

Genestra HMF Forte: two capsules upon rising

Biotics Bio-Doph 7: two capsules upon rising

Clear Flora (Clear Medicine): two capsules on rising

Ultra Flora (Metagenics): two capsules upon rising

Multi-Probiotic 4000 (Douglas Labs): two capsules on rising

If you are feeling a little bloated or upset digestively, try having a nice warm mug of either organic, peppermint, fennel, or ginger tea.

2.5 What Benefits Will I See And Feel From Clean Eating?

Clean, pure, low-allergen foods and drinks reduce the strain on the digestive tract because they come complete with the natural enzymes, vitamins and minerals that aid digestion. The longer you eat pure foods and give your digestive system a break, the greater the benefits will be. Your eyes will begin to regain their sparkle, your skin will appear clearer, and your hair will shine. Your intestinal bloating will reduce, meaning that your clothes won't feel tight and uncomfortable after a meal or at the end of the day, and your bowel movements will become calmer and more regular. The need for something sugary at the end of a meal should pass as your sugar levels stabilize and you feel more satiated after eating. You should also feel less tired after you've eaten.

Wahoo, doesn't this all sounds heavenly?!

2.6 Food Combining For Your Gut

It's not for everyone, but food combining is another great way to increase your digestive fire and ensure that you are assimilating more of what you eat. Each food has its own base of enzymes and Hydrochloric acid (HCL) in the stomach that it needs to break down, as well as its own transit time (eat-to-poop time).

When we combine our foods properly and in balance with each other, we remain energetic, happy, and satisfied from our meals. When we combine poorly or eat too much, we become filled with food that is literally just "hanging out" putrefying, fermenting, and building a lovely little internal bomb that will burn your butt and blow your friends away too!

You will also most likely become constipated and so

bloated that your pants will "suddenly" be too small! Right ... it's the pants that are the problem.

To help you decrease the nasty bloating, gas, and discomfort you have been feeling and help you lose weight PLUS increase your glow-factor, here are some Food Combining Fundamentals.

Food Combining Basics:

Eat <u>fruits</u> alone and allow thirty to sixty minutes before eating anything else with them.

<u>Starches</u> (grains, cereals, breads, beans, and starchy veggies) go great with vegetables and take roughly three to four hours to digest.

<u>Protein</u> (eggs, fish, chicken, meat, nuts, seeds, beans) goes great with vegetables, and also take roughly four hours to digest. NOTE: Animal flesh may take six to eight plus hours to be fully digested.

<u>Protein</u> and <u>Starch</u> do NOT combine well. Examples: pasta and meatballs, steak and potatoes, and eggs and toast.

<u>Protein</u> and <u>Fruit</u> do not combine well and neither do <u>Starch</u> and <u>Fruit</u>.

Certain foods like avocados and veggies are neutral and go with EVERYTHING!

Although fruits and veggies should be eaten alone, you can still juice and make smoothies with them together, as most find they are much more palatable and digestible this way.

Not All Fabulous People Are Created Equally!

This strategy may not work best for you, especially if you suffer from major low blood-sugar issues. Try it out for a day or two and see how you feel. If you notice any dizziness, nausea, or down-right crankiness, then add a little protein to your carbs and to your fresh fruit. Examples include:

Two tbsp raw nuts and seeds, small bit of goat cheese or feta, little bit of fish or shrimp, Greek yogurt etc.

Cheers to less bloating, belching, and you know what! Eat well, be well, and feel AMAZING.

Love to your bellies!

2.7 Your Liver Is Screaming For A Cleaning!

You eat to live and love to eat, but if your meals are mainly made up of processed, chemical-laden "foodstuffs", you aren't living your best, or up to your true potential.

What Is Your Liver Saying?

Some common signs of sluggish liver function are:

- Do you have poor tolerance or strong reaction to coffee, alcohol, and other stimulants?
- Do you have headaches and brain fog, especially in the morning?
- Do you have excess burping or indigestion after eating?
- Do you suffer from constipation, diarrhoea, or have light coloured stools?
- Do you find it difficult losing weight even when you watch what you eat?
- Do you have difficulty losing belly fat that is above your waistband? Women might feel their bra getting uncomfortable at their ribcage by the end of the day!

- Do you have high cholesterol?
- Do you have pressure or pain under the right ribcage, right shoulder, or shoulder blade?
- Do you suffer from eczema, acne, or psoriasis?
- Do you have a pattern of waking at night between 2:00 a.m. and 4:00 a.m.? You might feel irritable, agitated, or even notice your heart rate is a little higher at this time as well.

Now that you have a better understanding of your digestive system and why it's so important, it is time to introduce you to your LIVER!

Other than your skin (yes, that is an organ), your liver is the largest organ in your body weighing in at three to three and a half pounds; it has an incredibly broad range of critical functions in the body, which is why you really can't live without it.

It lies under your right lower rib cage and is only separated from your right lung by your main breathing muscle, the diaphragm.

The liver's many functions include: optimizing your metabolism by processing, storing or making protein, fat and carbohydrates; making cholesterol and triglycerides; synthesizing proteins and hormones for proper blood clotting and blood pressure; breaking down circulating hormones for excretion; producing bile for fat digestion; and detoxifying the entire body's system from chemical, medication, or other ingested toxins ... just to name a few!

Basically, the liver is a MASSIVE part of reaching your goals of healthy weight and overall vitality. It can be your body's BFF when beautifully aligned and functioning well, OR it can be a huge pain in the @** and energy-sucker if you continually overburden it and decrease its ability to function. If overburdened, it will result in pulling you and your health down with chronic, common, and persistent symptoms that never seem to go away!

So what can you do to improve the function of your liver? We will get to that in a moment, but first we need to teach you:

2.8 Becoming BFF's With Your Butt!

All right, be prepared to be uncomfortable with our topic for the next few minutes; it's a whole lot of SHIT ... we all have it and we all do it!

If you were to be completely honest, how often do you have a bowel movement? Well, if it's not at least one to three times daily, preferably after or in-between each meal you have consumed, then you my friend, are constipated!

There are quite possibly days, maybe even weeks of waste sitting in your guts putrefying, fermenting, and rotting away. I believe NASTY is the word you are looking for!

It doesn't matter how healthy your diet is, if your intestinal tract and system is backed up and plugged up, your body will begin to become toxic and break down. You will also have a difficult time getting rid of the gas, bloating, and excess weight you are carrying around, since it is all jammed up within twenty-eight feet of your intestines. How much "poop weight" do you think you could be carrying around?

Did you know that roughly 70% of your immune system is in your digestive tract, starting with your lymphatic system and ending with your butt? You have these tiny, yet very important, little villi that line the walls of your intestine and are responsible for absorbing nutrients out of your food. When they become damaged from leftover waste and toxins, their ability to take in the goodies from your food is greatly impaired, and in some cases doesn't happen at all, e.g., Celiac disease.

Your immune system is like your internal Warrior Flow series from yoga. It works synergistically with your breath, good bacteria, and movement to reduce and kill off any bad bacteria, parasites, and junk that eats through your food, water, and environment. The body needs a balance of the good bacteria and the bad bacteria in order to keep things in check. When there is too much bad bacteria through antibiotics, the birth control pill, corticosteroid creams, processed foods, too many animal products, dairy and sugar, the bad bacteria spreads, multiplies, and creates big problems.

All probiotics improve the balance of the intestinal microflora. Research has found that these live microorganisms are immune-enhancing and anti-inflammatory, and some studies have indicated they may protect against certain cancers. Probiotics prevent infections and yeast overgrowth by blocking harmful bacteria from attaching to intestinal walls and by maintaining intestinal pH. They improve digestive function and assist with the production of a number of vitamins, including vitamins K, B12, B5, and biotin.

So how can you keep the good bacteria strong and kick the bad guys out? Following your Simplicity Project eating guidelines; including more fibre, fresh fruits, and veggies; drinking two to three litres of pure water daily, etc. will help in a big way, but you also need to incorporate probiotics (good bacteria) into your daily regimen. There are many doctors, even some nutritionists and big commercial companies who will try to convince you that by simply adding yogurt to your everyday routine, you will be getting enough probiotics to do just this. However, most people who have digestive, intestinal or yeast issues and need to take probiotics, already have an issue with too much dairy and sugar (like that yogurt), so supplementing is a much more effective and concentrated way to get the probiotics you need.

Some great brands that I love are:

- Genuine Health Live probio + o3mega
- Genestra HMF Forte: two capsules upon rising
- Biotics Bio-Doph 7: two capsules upon rising
- Clear Flora (Clear Medicine): two capsules on rising
- Ultra Flora (Metagenics): two capsules upon rising
- Multi-Probiotic 4000 (Douglas Labs): two capsules on rising

Back To Your Lovely Little Liver!

So now that you know what your liver is responsible for and why it is so important to keep it free and clean, here are some extra steps you can take to give it a good washing from the inside out:

Begin every morning with a mug of warm water, half a fresh lemon juiced, a teaspoon of raw honey, and optionally a dash of cayenne.

Add chlorophyll to your water throughout the day.

Herbs like milk thistle, dandelion, turmeric, artichoke and/or beet leaf are fantastic and can be found separately or in liver detox combinations. These herbs improve the flow of bile and aid liver function.

Indole-3-carbinol helps to support liver cleansing, particularly the breakdown of harmful excess steroid hormones like estrogen and testosterone. A typical dose is 200 to 400 mg daily and it can be used for up to three months.

Teach Your Liver How To SMILE

According to many alternative health practitioners and researchers, the fix for liver problems could be as simple as repeating certain affirmations or "corrective thought patterns" to overwrite the problematic angry thoughts—essentially cancelling them out and replacing the harmful effects of these emotions with the more healing, beneficial chemistry of healthier thinking.

Louise Hay, in her book, *Heal Your Body*, recommends several affirmations for liver health, including:

"Love, Peace, and Joy are what I know."

"I choose to live through the open space in my heart. I look for love and find it everywhere."

"My mind is cleansed and free. I leave the past and move into the new. All is well."

"I feel tolerance, compassion, and love for all people—myself included."

"There is joyous release of the past. Life is sweet and so am I."

The simplicity of *The Simplicity Project* is that after a very short period of time, you won't be occupied with thoughts or feelings of constipation, diarrhoea, bloating, gas, or asking yourself the question, "Does my liver need a cleaning?"

You are now one step closer to feeling your best and looking amazing, from the inside out!

Let the TP (toilet paper) flow!

CHAPTER 3

YOUR FOOD.
YOUR MOOD.
YOUR ATTITUDE.

3.1 The Ultimate Balancing Act

This may be the very point, if it hasn't happened already, where you are beginning to feel overwhelmed with checking off the areas of imbalance in your body, reading more about the strong connection and impact between your digestion, gut and butt AND thinking to yourself, "Holy crap, this is going to be too much work! Where do I even begin?"

You begin here and now.

What I hope you're beginning to realize is that if you feel like you've been doing "everything" to lose weight and not succeeding, the problem may not be lack of effort or discipline on your part. It may be lack of knowing exactly what to do for YOUR body to shift into a weight and state that feels good and natural.

Don't rush the process; stick with me and take it slowly.

You may read and re-read this book a few times, or even for a few months before you feel ready to take some real steps—but they will come. You have to tell yourself that this is the beginning of a NEW YOU and YOU are so worth the wait.

This is where we start to dig deeper … a lot deeper.

If there is one aspect of your new regimen to remember, it is this: "Keep your blood sugar balanced." I truly believe if we all eat in a way that keeps our blood sugar balanced throughout the day, we will no longer have diseases or conditions like type 2 diabetes, insulin resistance, obesity, extreme cases of PMS, headaches, fatigue, bowel issues, etc. We can usually trace the cause to poor blood sugar control.

3.2 Your Blood Sugar—Your Food, Your Mood & Attitude

Tell me if this sounds familiar:

You wake up, make a coffee or two that you drink, maybe dump, re-heat, or repeat half way through, as you run around the house in the morning getting ready. You don't have time to make anything to eat, so you either go without breakfast (there are beans in coffee, right? LOL) or you stop at a local coffee shop or the work cafeteria and grab another coffee. You decide to get something to go with that coffee, such as a bagel with cream cheese, low-fat muffin, breakfast sandwich, or a super healthy lemon poppyseed loaf, and begin your day.

It's now around 10:00 a.m. or 11:00 a.m. and you are starting to feel a little hungry. You grab another coffee or maybe this time tea (there's just as much caffeine in tea) and indulge in a treat that a colleague brought in, or you have a piece of fruit, maybe a low fat yogurt, or nothing at all ... it's lunch time soon!

Note: At this point you are also acutely aware of the fact that your energy surge from your "super" morning breakfast is starting to fade, your cravings are beginning to say "Hello!", and you are now fantasizing about what you will "treat" yourself to for lunch!

Lunchtime!

Alrighty, let's see what I feel like? Hmmm ... two choices: boring salad you brought with lettuce, cucumber, tomatoes and cubed cheddar cheese with Italian dressing, and an apple for desert, OR maybe I will just run out for something quick (a.k.a. food through a window, such as pizza or a sub with all the fixings). Oh, plus my diet pop or iced tea—can't forget that!

Fast forward to somewhere between 1:00 p.m. to 3:30 p.m.

Wow! I am soooo tired, and ugh, all of a sudden my pants aren't fitting right; no one can see if I just unbutton the top, I'm at my desk.

But man alive, I could seriously take a nap right now and why is everyone around me becoming so annoying and loud and needy? I could totally go for a chocolate bar or chips right now, maybe another coffee or soda. I have enough time before bed; the caffeine won't keep me up all night.

Dinner Time!

By this point you are beyond starving, and as you are preparing dinner, IF you haven't already grabbed something on the way home, in your ravenous state you annihilate your cupboards and fridge looking for something—anything—to eat while you make dinner. So essentially, you are eating a meal while you prepare your meal. You then eat your pre-pared meal and have now consumed twice as many calories as you truly need.

Post Dinner

There's no way that I have the energy to work out now, too tired, but I could really go for a little something. You're not really hungry, but you would love a little treat. You've worked hard all day and the kids are finally in bed. You now get the chance to sit down, maybe watch a show and unwind. A few cookies, a little ice cream, or maybe some popcorn would be great.

Pre-Bed

You stand in front of the mirror and look at yourself asking, "Why did I eat what I did today?" That's it, tomorrow is a brand new day and I am going to change!

If this sounds at all familiar to you, even in part, I am so glad you came upon this book.

The above scenario is the perfect combination to create major blood sugar issues, gain extra weight, have no energy or motivation, and feel like you are simply dragging yourself through your days. This is not how you want to live and this will NEVER allow you to achieve your goals of losing weight and feeling great.

The General Rules Of BSB—Blood Sugar Balance

Eat within one hour of waking.

Eat every three to four hours thereafter, equalling roughly three meals and two snacks daily.

With each meal and snack, ensure that you are having a source of protein, carbohydrate, and fat, creating a balance of the three.

Getting the skinny on proteins, carbs, and fats will help you to understand why the Simplicity lifestyle is so effective.

Protein: Because protein feeds your muscles, consuming an adequate amount, especially while exercising, is crucial in maintaining your blood sugar and transforming your body. A diet with adequate protein will allow your muscles to grow, and in exchange, your body will be burning more calories and fat. So never skimp on protein. A healthy diet will include lean proteins, which you'll find in abundance in the meal and snack options I've provided in the meal plan. These include organic eggs, organic chicken and turkey, wild sustainable fish, dairy alternatives, tempeh, beans, raw nuts, seeds, and spirulina.

Fat: Fat has received a bad rap for decades, but we now have a better understanding that there are good fats and bad fats. Good fats are your essential fatty acids that contribute to the health of your hair, skin, nails, brain, quite literally every cell in your body; PLUS they help to keep your skin rich in moisture. They include avocados, raw nuts and seeds, olive oil, coconut oil, and grapeseed oil. On the not-so-good side, bad fats, a.k.a. saturated and hydrogenated fats, are those found in red meat, pork, full-fat cheese, cow's milk, highly processed baked goods, crackers, chips, cookies, and the list goes on. Now that you have seen the word hydrogenated, you will notice it in much of what is on the shelves in the supermarket, maybe even in your pantry.

Carbohydrates: Carbohydrates are essential to any well-balanced meal plan and way of life. Carbohydrates provide fuel for your brain and are responsible for replacing glycogen (your body's preferred source of fuel) in your muscles and liver. I think it is ludicrous when I see programs that eliminate carbs or drastically restrict them. However, keep in mind that an excess of carbs, and the wrong type, will increase your body's production of insulin and will be held onto by the body and stored as fat. The key with carbs is not to eliminate them—that's just not realistic or sustainable, and your weight loss won't last once you start to incorporate them back into your way of eating. Instead, select low-calorie, less wheat-based options like ancient grains such as quinoa, brown rice, kamut and spelt, whole fruits, fresh vegetables, beans and lentils.

In the following chapters, you will see how these suggestions play out over the course of a day when you are ready to begin sampling from the meal plan.

3.3 The New 'CISS'—Cortisol, Insulin, Sugar, Stress

These four demons are the main culprits behind our raging hormones, erratic moods, blemished skin, insomnia, uncomfortable digestion, bulging bellies, and more junk-in-the-trunk-than-our-pants-can-handle butts.

Cortisol (for more information on how we produce cortisol, refer to The Thyroid & Adrenal Connection in 3.4)

Unlike adrenalin produced by the adrenals, which draws on your fat stores for energy during stress, cortisol eats up your lean muscle tissue for fuel instead. Persistent stress will lead to muscle wasting and unstable blood sugar levels simply because your body is trying desperately to adapt. When your body gets to this state your levels of stress become extremely detrimental to the overall balance of your hormones, the ability to maintain a healthy weight and your day-to-day wellness in general.

High cortisol creates these negative impacts on your metabolism:

- It suppresses your metabolic process by interfering with your thyroid

- It makes you crave more sugary, processed, and fatty foods

- It increases the amount of weight you store around your waist

- It depletes serotonin, your happy, feel-good hormone, leading to depression, over-eating, and insane cravings

- It creates blood sugar imbalances like hypoglycemia

- It contributes to an increase in PMS and its intensity, along with headaches and moodiness

- It increases a hormone called NPY (neuropeptide Y), which increases your appetite. Then it decreases the hormone, leptin, which tells your body you are satisfied. Translation—you don't recognize when to stop eating

Too much cortisol also screws up your circadian rhythm and leads to major sleep issues, a huge culprit in weight gain.

Cortisol also decreases your body's receptivity to insulin and greatly contributes to insulin resistance, type 2 diabetes, Polycystic Ovarian Syndrome (PCOS), and infertility.

If your stress continues and your cortisol levels stay elevated, you will end up with a raging appetite, death to your metabolism, a mega buddha-belly, and the loss of any metabolically active lean muscle tissue that you are working so hard to achieve with your exercise.

So how do you balance it out?

You follow your Simplicity Project "On My Way To Feeling Awesome" checklist like it is your J.O.B. You can find this in section 10.1.

You also consider adding in these supplements to support you:

1. Refer to Chapter 8 and begin using your daily recommended supplements

2. Ashwagandha — this is an herb that works as a general tonic to support the adrenals. It can also help with feelings of being overwhelmed, broken sleep, and like you're on a hamster wheel that won't stop running. Average dose is between 500 and 1,000 mg taken two times daily for at least two to six months for full benefits.

3. Holy Basil — an amazing herb to use when hypoglycemia and insulin resistance are also suspected. It is an adaptogen that helps the body handle and cope with stress more effectively. Take two gel caps per day for at least one month.

4. Relora — this supplement is a mixture of two herbs and works beautifully to reduce cortisol and increase Dehydroepiandrosterone (DHEA). It is recommended to take 250 mg, three times daily.

There are a few good combination products on the market today as well: Lorna Vanderhaege has a complete line, Genuine Health, St. Francis, Biotics Research, and Clear Medicine are just a few.

Okay, now what can you do to stop this vicious cycle?

In combination with all of the other recommendations

throughout this book, a great place to start is by truly understanding what contributes to excess insulin, and making shifts in your diet and lifestyle.

There are some good supplements to consider as well:

1. CLA (Conjugated Linoleic Acid) — one of few supplements proven to lower body fat and to help increase lean muscle without any changes to overall calories. This is due to its insulin-sensitizing properties and the fact that it helps to reduce inflammation. Recommended dose is 1600 mg, two times daily for at least three to four months.

2. Holy Basil — as recommended above, this herb will help reduce cortisol levels, improve blood sugar balance, and the use of insulin in the body. Recommended dose is two gel caps daily. Try this dosage for three months with a one month rest and see what you notice. If you feel a difference, then repeat this same cycle.

3. Chromium Picolinate — is a mineral involved in regulating blood sugar by helping the body's response to insulin. Recommended dose is 200 to 400 mcg (microgram) daily. If your glucose levels are showing signs of pre-diabetes, increase to 1000 mcg daily, for six months.

Sugar

Sugar was once called "white death".

It deserves 100 percent of this title. It is a key factor in most degenerative diseases, and in order for us as a society to get control over our health, we must stop consuming it.

On some level most of us know that sugar is not healthy, but the majority of us truly have no idea how devastating sugar really is.

Can you believe the world's consumption of sugar, or processed carbohydrate that converts to sugar, is estimated at about 10 to 200 pounds each year by the average Western person? It is estimated that sugar constitutes about 25 to 35 percent of the Western diet.

You can put your eyes back in your head now.

What you need to watch for:

Simple carbohydrates: These can be metabolized quickly and are therefore most likely to cause an insulin surge. Simple carbohydrates include the various forms of sugar, such as sucrose (table sugar), fructose (fruit sugar), lactose (dairy sugar), and glucose (blood sugar). Watch for the "ose" ending.

Hidden sugar in processed foods: Watch for hidden sugar in processed foods like bread, ketchup, salad dressing, canned fruit, applesauce, peanut butter, and soups.

Sugar in beverages: Be aware of the amount of sugar in beverages, especially specialty coffees and soda pop. It can add up quickly, and most of these types of drinks aren't filling.

Fat-free products: Sugar is often used to replace the flavour that is lost when the fat is removed. And as if that's not bad enough, without any fat to slow it down, the sugar is absorbed into your blood faster.

Cereal box claims of less sugar: Many newer cereals do contain less sugar, but the calories, carbohydrates, fat, fibre and other nutrients are almost identical to the full-sugar cereals. The manufacturers have simply replaced sugar with other refined, simple carbohydrates.

No sugar added: It doesn't mean that the product doesn't naturally contain a lot of sugar; 100 percent fruit products often contain concentrated fruit juice, still another form of fructose or sugar.

Table sugar (sucrose) is often said to provide empty calories because it has no nutritional value other than providing fuel for energy. Honey, maple syrup, brown rice syrup, molasses, and other more natural sugars, on the other hand, are often considered to be healthier because of the trace vitamins and minerals they provide. They are still SUGAR! For weight loss purposes, all of these sweeteners can simply be treated as sugar.

Sugar-free: This almost always means that it contains an artificial sweetener such as sucralose, aspartame, saccharin and all chemical and unnatural sweeteners.

I HAVE ZERO TOLERANCE FOR ARTIFICIAL SWEETENERS

All of these are highly damaging neurotoxins and excitotoxins that do nothing but destroy your body at the deepest and most intrinsic level.

Even moderate use is linked to:

- Headaches and migraines
- Change in vision
- Increased heart rate
- Depression
- Weight gain and the inability to lose weight
- Increase in cravings
- Nausea and vomiting
- Insomnia/sleep problems
- Abdominal and joint pain
- Memory loss

- Seizures

- Brain cancer and bladder cancer

- Demyelination of your nerve axons

Every nerve in your body is coated by a protective sheath called myelin. When artificial sweeteners are present in the body, they destroy this essential sheath exposing the nerve axons. Without this protective coating, your nerves will begin to be destroyed, little by little, by the floating free radicals circulating in your body. Your nerve axons will be literally picked away by the free radicals until permanent damage is done to them, affecting the overall communication and function of your entire nervous system.

Pay attention to the people around you that use a lot of artificially sweetened products, e.g., diet pop, gum, yogurt, juice, candies, baked goods, jams, pudding, gelatin, etc. Do they look, sound, or feel healthy, happy, in good shape, or maintaining a healthy body weight? Or do they look puffy, tired, stiff and overweight? Do they always seem to be on a diet, frequently get headaches or sick, and have general aches and pains all the time? Plus, do they seem ADDICTED to their diet stuff?

This little observation should be enough to give you the right information as to whether or not eating this "stuff" is good for you. Is it going to help you lose weight and feel great, OR is it is going to keep you where you are with your weight and feeling not-so-great?

Stress

Stress is like an internal bomb to your hormones—even just a small amount can act like an explosion of craziness.

If you stay in stress mode long enough, those precious adrenals and your über-important thyroid will frazzle right before your eyes.

Stress can also contribute to:

- Leptin resistance
- Insulin resistance
- Lower estrogen in women
- Lower growth hormone
- Higher cortisol levels
- Depression and mood disorders
- Mega PMS

Every single one of these will slow down your metabolism and cause you to gain weight.

Try some of these techniques to help better manage your stress:

- Eat according to *The Simplicity Project*
- Keep a journal next to your bed. If you can't sleep because your mind is going a mile a minute, sit up and write it down. Get it off your chest and out of your head
- Learn to meditate even if it's for five minutes per day with your eyes closed, body still, and breath focused. You will be amazed at how incredible you feel
- Practice yoga. Not only is it a dynamic way to move every muscle in your body, it also lowers your stress by having you focus on setting a "groundation", being in the breath and then letting the movement shine through

- Get a massage, a facial, or some form of spa treatment to unwind

- Take a vacation. Did you know that working in excess of forty hours per week more than doubles your risk of depression, obesity, and heart disease?[5] Try to take some time away at least every few months, even if it's only for a few days

We all need to get more rest and master the technique of chilling out!

3.4 The Thyroid & Adrenal Connection

Why Your Thyroid Doesn't Give A Crap If You're Tired, Over-Worked, Not Exercising, Blah Blah Blah ...

The reason your thyroid no longer gives a crap about your complaints is because it no longer hears you, no longer responds to you, and can no longer pick your butt up off the couch and do the work you need it to do anymore. You have obliterated it.

After years of yo-yo dieting; drinking sugary instant weight loss shakes or doing blender diets; taking diet pills; getting poor sleep; not exercising; falling asleep at the TV; taking no supplements (or poor quality supplements that have bogged down your liver and are now interfering with your endocrine system); stressing about the most insignificant things; making everyone else's problem your own; not having enough sex; eating within three hours of going to bed; going to bed past 10:00 p.m. or 10:30 p.m.; enjoying more than one cup of coffee daily; drinking cow's milk; eating loads of wheat, sugar, and Genetically Modified Foods (GMOs); and taking medication and getting vaccines regularly—you may have trouble finding true joy in your life, and have about as much energy, and feel about as amorous as a piece of wood.

Describe Anyone You Know???

I get it. You feel overwhelmed with your schedule or too stressed out. You feel like every time you make an effort, you don't see results. You don't think you have the money to exercise or eat healthy.

Well, guess what? Suck it up! Stop using every excuse in the book for why you CAN'T and start shifting that energy and changing your language to why you CAN, and more importantly, why you NEED to!

You're feeling overwhelmed? Sit down and look at your schedule. How much are you committed to? Why? Do you need to be doing all of these things? How many activities are your kids involved in? Do they need to be doing so many things? How do you think their bodies are coping? Have you sat down and asked them what they want to do? Can you share the responsibility of driving kids to activities with other parents? How many things in your life are you simply saying yes to because you don't think you have a choice? Really?! Who is in charge of your life, your joy?

I have to reassess my busy schedule every couple of months or I get terribly out of balance. It's very easy to say yes to everything that looks great or sounds important, but how many of these activities decrease your health and vitality as opposed to contribute to it?

When it comes to exercise and eating right, have you done everything and put in tons of effort, but have seen no results? Really? Are you being completely honest with yourself? Have you tried EVERYTHING and nothing has worked, OR have you tried something for a few days or maybe a week and nothing has worked? Huge difference.

Here is my general rule: If you are in your twenties, give yourself two solid months of commitment before you complain that nothing is happening. If you are in your thirties, give yourself three solid months; in your forties, you guessed it, allow four solid months. When you are fifty and beyond, it needs to be a daily routine for creating longevity, and we should all be moving at least thirty minutes, five or more days per week.

You don't think you can afford to exercise? Last time I checked, walking, jogging, squatting, push-ups, lunges, tricep dips, planks, crunches, and biking were all free.

Eating healthy is too expensive for me? My family purchases all whole foods, largely organic and non-GMO. I shop two times per week: once for the whole shebang and another time for extra produce. My grocery bills are far less than most of my friends, colleagues, and family members. How is that possible, you ask? I PLAN. I create a meal plan, I shop based solely on that meal plan and I prepare dishes that will serve for two meals. I get very creative and we eat smaller portions. We eat until we are satisfied and content, not until we are full. The result: we are all maintaining healthy body weights, energy levels, sleep patterns (our four-year-old son, Sam, is a work-in-progress), and we're not passing out on the couch for a nap or losing our mind with low blood sugar.

More importantly, when I look at my children it teaches me a ton and keeps me motivated. Emerson, my six-year-old daughter, is a fabulous eater but LOVES her sweets. If I let her, she would have a treat every hour of the day. However, I don't and she knows it. She is beginning to recognize that when she eats treats on special occasions, they taste great but she feels crummy after. Sam becomes hell on wheels if he has sugar. He will then tell me that his treat made him crazy and sad. LOL.

Do You Know What Your Thyroid Is Actually Responsible For?

Well, it performs a ton of different activities: it helps control the amount of oxygen each cell uses, the rate at which you burn calories, your heart rate, body temperature, fertility, digestion, memory, sex drive, energy and your mood—basically, the whole deal.

When your thyroid is out of whack, too high or too low, chemical and hormonal reactions throughout your whole body get thrown off. An under-active thyroid is like death to your metabolism, and you will watch in frustration as the weight keeps packing on.

Some years ago in my holistic nutrition practice I began to notice a pattern: thyroid dysfunction was really common in my stressed-out clients. Though I hadn't spent much time on this relationship in my initial trainings, I felt, as a female practitioner caring for women of all ages, shapes, and walks of life, I should start to pay more attention to this connection. And the more I learned, the more I realized there is a very tight physiological connection between a woman's thyroid function and her stress response.

Yes, we all know stress isn't good for our health, but we don't always make the connection between stress and thyroid problems, or how to change our lives in response. Continuous stress leads to high levels of stress hormones, which will have a negative impact on thyroid function, especially if levels stay high over the long-term.

This inhibition of your thyroid and hormone receptors often takes place quietly behind the scenes for years without causing overt symptoms. And this is why so many women are caught off-guard when they are diagnosed with a thyroid disorder. They think everything has been going fine and all of a sudden, they feel horrible. The fact is, if you've been experiencing chronic stress, stress hormones may have been inhibiting your thyroid function for years. Some patients can even remain in what we call *subclinical hypothyroidism*, where their lab results are still within the standard normal ranges, but they're experiencing symptoms.

Thankfully, there are many ways to reset your stress response and re-establish communication along your adrenal–thyroid pathways.

So What Can You Do?

As recommended previously:

- eliminate junk food; anything that is processed, refined, contains white sugar, hydrogenated oil, high fructose corn syrup, MSG
- stop drinking cow's milk and switch to milk alternatives such as almond, coconut, hemp, flax or rice.
- No SOY!!!
- Cook your goitrogenic, cruciferous foods such as broccoli, cauliflower etc. (P.S. Please do not tell me you have an underactive thyroid because you have eaten too many veggies.)
- And, of course, eat within one hour of waking.
- Eat every three to four hours, small balanced meals made up of real food.
- Carb, protein, fat at each meal.

- Drink two litres of water daily. Stop using plastic bottles; they are massively screwing up your thyroid! Choose glass or stainless steel.

- Drink no more than one cup of coffee or black tea daily. Choose herbal teas.

- Stop eating within three hours of going to bed.

- To keep your core body temperature down at night, keep the bedroom cool and don't wear warm clothing.

- Sleep in complete darkness and turn off lights, TV, mobile phones and computers by 10:00 p.m. or 10:30 p.m. Your best sleep will be obtained between 10:30 p.m. and 6:30 a.m.

- Exercise for thirty to sixty minutes, five to six days per week: strength train two times weekly, yoga two times weekly, and cardio two times weekly.

- Exercise is wonderful, but over-exercising can also stress your thyroid and over-stimulate your adrenal glands resulting in elevated cortisol levels, so pace yourself.

- Counter your daily stress. There are many ways—some requiring more of a commitment than others—to help your body relax, from deep breathing exercises to scheduling a massage or spa day.

- Throw out all of your cosmetics, body products, and regular feminine hygiene products that are laden with chemicals such as parabens, sodium laureate sulfate, PEG 70, perfumes, dyes, etc. Most commercial products on the market today are pure chemicals, and will MASSIVELY affect not only your thyroid but EVERY SINGLE CELL in your body. I cannot stress this enough.

- And Moms, get your children off these chemically-laden products too. You don't want them to ever have to feel like you do right now.

- Consider instead, Cocoon Apothecary, Burt's Bees, Say Yes To Carrots, Aubrey, Green Beaver or Mineral Fusion.

- Switch to iodized salt.

- Add 5,000 IU of vitamin D, omega 3 fatty acids, a complete B complex with a 2,000 mcg extra vitamin B12 in a sublingual form, selenium, zinc and your probiotics daily. Additional supplements and/or herbs may be recommended based on a personal consultation with a qualified practitioner.

Consult your family doctor, or better yet a Naturopathic doctor, to get your levels tested properly. Western medicine measurements suggest that anything in the range of 5.2 to 5.5 is worrisome. In the holistic medicine world, we get alarmed if we see anything at 2.0 or above. The goal is to discover when the thyroid is functioning sub-optimally, before it's not functioning at all.

If you need medication, discuss this with a naturopath as there may be ways to use bio-identical medication to help you too.

I can at times come across as harsh, to the point, and with little sympathy. I don't have sympathy for you, I have HOPE for you!

I have been at this long enough to know that: a) you are hard-pressed for time and you want the info and the plan now, and b) sweet, gentle talk accomplishes one thing—the chance for you to come up with more excuses.

The Adrenals: Your Body's SWAT Team In Response To Stress

Fatigue is one of the most common symptoms I hear about from my clients and students. When I ask women to tell me about what's going on in their lives, all too often the answers reveal they have more responsibility than appears humanly possible to manage.

They're waking up still tired; unable to think straight without caffeine; need high-carb snacks, additional caffeine, or naps to get through the afternoon; then they burn the midnight oil because they're too wired to sleep. Alcohol or sleep aids are sometimes used to unwind, which can disrupt normal sleep patterns, and set them up for non-refreshing sleep. Pretty soon, they're caught in a seemingly unending cycle of exhaustion and poor nutrition, desperate for the energy and vigour they once had.

Tiny In Size, Massive In Responsibility

Your adrenal glands are tiny in comparison to many other organs—each is roughly the size of a walnut—yet they have enormous responsibilities in your body. When they are functioning properly, these small glands help you feel energized when you need to be, and relaxed when it is time for rest. They produce cortisol and Dehydroepiandrosterone (DHEA), and contribute to the production of estrogen, testosterone, progesterone, and so much more. But life's demands can slowly drain the balancing power and stamina of the adrenal glands. Even the healthiest person's adrenals become out of balance under chronic, persistent stress.

Our body's stress response—when the adrenals produce the hormone cortisol—is a normal and necessary function.

We need cortisol to handle emergencies. However, the stress response is designed to be short-term, with a fairly quick return to a relaxed state of being.

Unfortunately, our adrenals don't know the difference between a true emergency and the stress from our jobs, relationships, finances, body weight, etc. Many of us stay revved up all day in a fight-or-flight state. But when cortisol stays elevated like that, our bodies gradually become less sensitive to the mechanism that helps bring it back to normal and allows us to chill out.

Cortisol Gone Wrong

If your cortisol levels remain elevated more days than not in your life, there are some pretty major physical repercussions you need to know about and definitely try to avoid!

High levels of cortisol will contribute to:

- Impaired digestion and sluggish bowel a.k.a constipation
- Depressed immunity
- Insomnia and varying sleep issues — the classic issue is waking between 2:00 a.m. and 4:00 a.m. and unable to get back to sleep
- Hormonal imbalances
- Weight gain around your waist and the backs of your upper arms and face
- High blood pressure and resting heart
- Unstable blood sugar making you more susceptible to cravings, mood swings and more likely to develop insulin resistance and possibly type 2 diabetes

- Increased inflammation — joint and muscle aches and pains, skin problems

- Adrenal dysfunction — remember that your adrenals are what help your body respond to and COPE with stress. If they become out of balance, YOU become out of balance and feel majorly overwhelmed

- ZERO sex drive — ☹

Phew ... I am exhausted and uncomfortable just writing about all that can go wrong when cortisol is not properly balanced ... now imagine feeling like the above ALL THE TIME! This is unfortunately how many people are living.

Okay, now to pick you up and make you smile and excited again!

We can, YOU can heal this! It all comes down to how badly do you want to FEEL the change? Are you willing to change what you are eating, when you are eating and how you are preparing or eating it? Are you willing to make some shifts and adjustments in your lifestyle and patterns for a healthier, sassier-feeling you?

Through proper, healthy and supportive eating, specific exercise and lymphatic stimulation, great restorative sleep, managing your stress, a solid supplement regimen, better sex, embracing your breath and finding/creating more joy ... in a nutshell, if you follow *The Simplicity Project* you will feel better than you have in years and everyone else, including Miss Cortisol, will notice.

For now I would like all your energy and focus to be on understanding the importance of your blood sugar ... it is truly the key to it all.

Your thyroid is one of the most important organs in your body. It is your internal thermostat, responsible for your metabolic fire, proper digestion, hormone communication, and achieving and maintaining your ideal body weight. It gives you energy, helps you to maintain healthy bowels and regular function, helps to keep your fertility (both men and women) strong and healthy and the list goes on.

Never Let Your Blood Sugar Get Too Low

Long periods without food make the adrenals work harder by requiring them to release more cortisol and adrenalin to keep your body functioning normally. Eating three nutritious meals and two to three snacks throughout the day is one way to balance blood sugar and lessen the adrenal burden.

When you eat your meals and snacks can make a big difference as well. Cortisol follows a natural cycle that works with your circadian rhythm—your natural wake/sleep pattern. Normally, it begins to rise around 6:00 a.m. and reaches its highest peak around 8:00 a.m. Throughout the day, cortisol gradually and naturally declines, with small upward bumps at meal times, to prepare your body for night-time rest. That's why cortisol is normally at its lowest level during the night.

Ideally, you want to work with this natural cycle to keep the tapering-off of levels as smooth as possible as the day progresses, and to avoid dramatic ups and downs. Eating the majority of your food earlier in the day can help accomplish this; so can eating an early dinner (by 5:00 p.m. or 6:00 p.m.). If it's difficult for you to eat early, you can at least try to make your evening meal the lightest one of the day. Many of my clients tell me that overeating at dinner, and before bed, provides them with a sense of comfort at the end of their day. However, if our cortisol levels are still high at this time, we'll be attracted to foods that are high in sugar and fat. Unfortunately too, this eating habit often further upsets our hormone balance.

Keep in mind that cortisol will also rise a bit with exercise. Lighter activities, such as a walk after dinner or some gentle stretching, will not interrupt this natural tapering-off process. But to work in concert with your body's natural cortisol cycle, more intense exercise is best planned for the morning or early afternoon.

Pay attention and refer back to the recommendations I gave you for your thyroid, in section 3.4—The Thyroid and Adrenal Connection. In addition, consider these recommendations:

If possible, eat breakfast by 8:00 a.m. or within an hour of getting up (earlier is better), to restore blood sugar levels after your body has been relying on glycogen stores for energy during the night.

Eat a nutritious snack around 10:00 a.m. to soften the natural dip in cortisol that tends to happen late morning.

Try to eat lunch between 12:00 p.m. and 1:00 p.m. because your morning meal can be used up quickly.

Eat a nutritious snack between 2:45 p.m. and 3:30 p.m. to get you through the natural dip in cortisol around 3:00 p.m. or 4:00 p.m.

Make an effort to eat dinner by 6:00 p.m., and make this your lightest meal of the day. Try using a salad plate instead of your large dinner plate to control portion sizes.

Finally, if needed, eat a light and nutritious snack no later than three hours before bed. For example, an apple with a tbsp of raw cashews, half a cup Greek yogurt with four tbsp of hemp granola, or a pear with one tbsp of raw almond butter.

Supporting your body's natural rhythms by properly timing meals to prevent dramatic dips in blood sugar has lots of benefits: it minimizes cortisol output and frees up your adrenals to perform their secondary functions, and also gives you more sustained energy throughout the day. Life becomes much more enjoyable when you have the energy you need!

You have the power to lessen the burden on your adrenals and your whole body; it just takes consistency. The small choices you make daily in your lifestyle and eating patterns will make a big difference.

Soon you'll find the energy you thought was lost—and it will be back and here to stay!

3.5 Why Do Your Hormones Have Such Impact On All Aspects Of Your Being?

Seriously? You don't know the answer to this one yet?! LOL

Okay, here is the short answer.

Your hormones are messengers. They communicate and tell a story throughout your entire body. If one area, page of the story, or the content shifts for long enough, line after line, page after page, the whole story changes and the outcome is different. The key in any quest for health is to be consistent and diligent. Our bodies, specifically our hormones, like balance. Try it out and see how you feel.

CHAPTER 4

FANNING THE OUT-OF-CONTROL FLAMES—GETTING RID OF INFLAMMATION

4.1 Alkalize Your Body & Revitalize Your LIFE! pH 101

When it comes to your health, you're most likely trying to do a lot of things right: watching what you eat, exercising, and trying to reduce stress. However, there is often one major thing that we completely overlook. According to the latest research from both Western and alternative medicine, ultimate health can only be achieved with a balanced pH.

Potential hydrogen, or pH, represents the balance of positively charged (acid-forming) ions to negatively charged (alkaline-forming) ions in your body. The lower the pH of your blood, the more acidic; the higher the pH, the more alkaline.

The level of acidity in your body directly affects and impacts your overall health, including energy, digestion, weight and skin—as well as your risk for serious diseases such as cancer, osteoporosis, heart and stroke disease, and obesity.

For optimum health your pH should be slightly alkaline; however, the majority of people are overly acidic due to their unbalanced diets. The good news is that you can become more alkaline through a more nourishing real-food diet and improving upon your lifestyle habits.

This is something I learned about long ago, but until lately hadn't put a lot of everyday thought into it. I know for myself and my family that we eat well and are pretty balanced, so I've had no red flags to dive deeper into the whole acid/alkaline issue.

However, recently my Dad has had two surgeries and is on the mend, working hard at increasing his quality of living and doing a wonderful job. These experiences with him have caused some of my knowledge and training to resurface. As we all know, the more acidic your body is, the more inflammation you will have and suffer from. The key to reducing inflammation is reducing the foods you consume that produce an inflammatory response in your body.

Every day we receive energy and a steady flow of oxygen from the foods we eat. After food is eaten, it is broken down, digested, and absorbed. What's left behind is an ash residue that's either acidic—requiring your body to eliminate it through the intestines, kidneys, skin, or lungs—or it's alkaline. Before your body can excrete or eliminate the waste, it must neutralize it using a steady source of oxygen and organic minerals found in foods such as vegetables, sea vegetables, herbs, and green food supplements. When there are enough oxygen and alkaline minerals available for neutralization, the body's pH remains balanced and its organs function correctly.

Acidosis—the term used in an overly acidic body, happens when we consume too much food that is acid-forming like: peanut butter, sulphur-dried fruits, MSG, soya sauce, white vinegar, ketchup and pickles, alcohol, soft drinks, coffee, cookies, sweets and artificial sweeteners, white bread, flour, rice and pasta, red meat, pork and shellfish, etc. And when they outweigh the more alkalizing items like: fresh vegetables, fruit, Celtic sea salt, black olives, miso, bee pollen, raw seeds and nuts, sprouts, probiotics, etc., the body has to use its own "buffers" (stored alkalizing minerals) to neutralize the acidic load. Emotional and physical stress also increases the acidity due to their uric acid by-product.

What Happens When Your Body Is Too Acidic?

In addition to the most common signs such as low energy and poor digestion, studies show a direct link between acidic pH and a variety of health issues, including:

- premature aging
- inadequate absorption of vitamins and minerals
- low bone density/osteoporosis
- poor skin, hair, and nail health
- weight gain
- toxin build-up
- frequent cold, flu, and headache

Before we jump into why and how it can affect your weight, I think you may need a better understanding of what the body's recognition of food as acidic or alkaline actually means.

4.2 Not All Acidic Foods Are Created The Same

Considering whether a food is acidifying or alkalizing in the diet can require some mind-bending, because some foods that we think of as acidic are, in fact, alkalizing in the diet. It's actually better to look at whether the food is acid-forming or alkaline-forming, not where the food itself falls on the pH scale. So even though we think of citrus as acidic, fruits like lemons and tangerines are alkalizing because when they're consumed, they break down and donate alkaline mineral salt compounds like citrates and ascorbates. Similarly, foods we might normally think of as meek and mild in nature are acid-forming when ingested. Grains and milk are two examples.

What's important is not so much the pH of the food as it goes into our bodies, but the resultant pH once the food is broken-down, and this is dictated by the residues that the broken-down nutrients leave behind, particularly sulphates and phosphates.

Below is a reference guide that will hopefully help you to make better sense of what foods to consume more, and what foods to consume less.

You will notice that there are some very healthy foods on the acid side of things; it does not make them bad to eat. Remember there needs to be a balance between acidic and alkaline, not a dominance.

4.3 Your Alkaline vs. Acidic Reference Guide

ALKALIZING VEGETABLES

Alfalfa	Garlic	Peas
Barley grass	Green beans	Pumpkin
Beets and beet greens	Green peas	Radishes
Broccoli	Kale	Sea veggies
Cabbage	Kohlrabi	Spinach
Carrot	Lettuce	Sprouts
Cauliflower	Mushrooms	Sweet potatoes
Celery	Nightshade veggies	Wild greens
Cucumber	(tomatoes, peppers,	
Fermented veggies	eggplant, etc.)	
(sauerkraut, kim chee)	Onions	

ALKALIZING FRUITS

Apple	Figs, dried	Pear
Apricot	Grapes	Pineapple
Avocado	Grapefruit	Raisins
Banana	Honeydew melon	Raspberries
Berries	Lemon	Rhubarb
Cantaloupe	Lime	Strawberries
Cherries, sour	Muskmelons	Tangerine
Coconut, fresh	Nectarine	Tropical fruits
Currants	Orange	Watermelon
Dates, dried	Peach	

ALKALIZING PROTEIN

Almonds	Tempeh (fermented)	Whey protein
Chestnuts	Tofu (fermented)	powder
Millet		

OTHER ALKALIZING FOODS

Apple cider vinegar	Lecithin granules	Probiotic cultures
Bee pollen	Mineral water	Soured (cultured)
Green juices	Molasses, blackstrap	dairy products

ACIDIFYING VEGETABLES

Corn	Olives	Winter squash

ACIDIFYING FRUITS

Blueberries	Cranberries	Plums
Canned or glazed fruits	Currants	Prunes

ACIDIFYING GRAINS

Amaranth	Oatmeal	Rye
Barley	Quinoa	Spelt
Bread	Rice	Wheat
Corn		

ACIDIFYING BEANS AND LEGUMES

Black beans	Kidney beans	Red beans
Chick peas	Lentils	Soy beans
Green peas	Pinto beans	White beans

ACIDIFYING DAIRY

Butter	Ice cream
Cheese	Milk

ACIDIFYING NUTS

Cashews	Peanuts	Tahini
Legumes	Pecans	Walnuts

ACIDIFYING ANIMAL PROTEIN

Bacon	Lobster	Sausage
Beef	Mussels	Scallops
Carp	Organ meats	Shellfish
Clams	Oyster	Shrimp
Cod	Pike	Tuna
Corned beef	Pork	Turkey
Fish	Rabbit	Veal
Haddock	Salmon	Venison
Lamb	Sardines	

ACIDIFYING FATS AND OILS

Avocado oil	Flax oil	Safflower oil
Butter	Hemp seed oil	Sesame oil
Canola oil	Lard	Sunflower oil
Corn oil	Olive oil	

ACIDIFYING SWEETENERS

Carob	Corn syrup	Sugar

ACIDIFYING ALCOHOL

Beer	Spirits
Hard liquor	Wine

Now some of this may get a little "science-geekish" on you, but it's important to understand!

As food makes its way from your mouth to your stomach, the digestive tract becomes more acidic. Pepsin, the enzyme responsible for protein breakdown, needs an acidic environment and therefore gets released into the stomach, where pH is very low (about 2.0 to 1.5). Your small intestine is where most of the nutrients in your food get absorbed, and where the pH increases from 2.0 to 6.5 as the food travels from the stomach to the small and large intestines.

Protein, particularly in the form of red meats, requires huge amounts of alkaline minerals for complete digestive processing. When the system goes looking for the alkalinity needed to offset the acid load, it looks first to the minerals currently in the digestive tract. If it fails to find alkaline nourishment there, it draws on the calcium, magnesium, phosphorus and potassium minerals stored in our bones.

4.4 Have A Love Affair With Your Greens

This is where the healthy, "good for you" greens and essential vitamins and minerals come in. Instead of "making out" with your dirty, processed, junky foods, how about giving some lip service to your luscious greens!

When we eat a diet that is rich in nutrients, there's no need to draw on the stored minerals in the bones. It's when we don't consume a nutrient-rich diet, or worse, when we over consume foods that promote acidity in the body, that we start tapping our bone resources. In the short-term, this isn't an issue, but in the long run, it can have serious consequences, not just for our bone health but also for our overall health.

Dark green leafy vegetables are an excellent source of many vitamins, like vitamins A, C, K, and folate, and minerals such as iron and calcium. They're great sources of fibre as well. The nutrients found in dark green vegetables may prevent certain types of cancers and promote heart health. It is recommended that teenage girls eat three cups of dark green vegetables per week, or about half a cup every day. Adult women should be having double that!

Your body needs a little dietary fat to absorb some of the vitamins found in dark green vegetables. To accomplish this, simply add a bit of salad dressing or oil, such as olive, grapeseed, or coconut, if you are cooking; and flax, avocado, hemp, sesame, or safflower, if your vegetables are raw.

There Are A Variety Of Dark Leafy Greens To Choose From:

Arugula, collard greens, dandelion greens, kale, mustard greens, romaine lettuce, spinach, swiss chard, red chard, micro greens and sprouts.

Some Easy Ways To Incorporate More Greens Into Your Everyday Diet:

Try adding them into soups, stews, pastas, salads, wraps, sandwiches, omelettes, ratatouille, stir-frys, smoothies, or lightly steaming them and flavouring with olive oil, sea salt, garlic, ginger and a little goat cheese … yummy!

4.5 Enzymes: Your Metabolic Fire's Kindling For Life

Your enzymes are one of your most valuable assets, igniting more reactions in your cells throughout your entire body than you could ever imagine. There are literally thousands of different enzymes in your body, all with different roles and duties. Of those thousands, they're divided into two types of enzymes that you produce: digestive and metabolic.

Digestive enzymes break your food down into smaller, easier to digest particles so that your body can assimilate (absorb) the nutrients into your body and send them off where you need them most.

Digestion truly starts in the mouth within your saliva with amylase, the enzyme that begins breaking down starches into sugar. As your food makes its way down into your stomach, it is met by pepsin to help break down proteins and then onto lipase, an enzyme produced by the pancreas and released into your small intestine, to break down fats. If you don't have enough enzymes in your body or enough HCL (hydrochloric acid), complete digestion and proper assimilation cannot take place.

When this happens you often experience bloating, gas, upset bowels, and generally feel like crap. Most likely, your food is literally sitting there putrefying and fermenting, which is what causes all the bloating, gas, and discomfort.

Keep in mind: if you are not digesting the food you eat, you are also NOT able to fuel your body for metabolic purposes, to exercise, or to lose weight!

4.6 The Pure Power Of Eating More Living Raw Foods

Did you know that when you cook any of your foods, yes even your gorgeous greens and beautiful reds, oranges, and yellows, that you are destroying much of the nutrients and enzymes they provide to you?

The less enzyme energy your food has, the more it relies on your digestive system to help break it down. If your digestive system is low on enzymes then it can't do the job ... so you see where this is going? Yup, gas and indigestion-land!

In order for our cells to remain healthy, happy, and well, they need oxygen; they THRIVE on plant-based foods. When we cook our foods too much, boil them, microwave them, or eat too many animal products, refined foods, and chemicals, we deprive our cells of oxygen.

Do you know what hates oxygen? Cancer cells.

Cancer cells thrive in oxygen-devoid environments and CANNOT survive in an oxygen-rich, more alkaline environment.

Raw and living foods such as wheatgrass, dark leafy greens, veggies, sprouts, certain fruits, raw nuts and seeds, grains, seaweed, green juices, and smoothies literally saturate our bodies with nutrient-rich chlorophyll, vitamins, minerals, enzymes and phytonutrients.

4.7 Give Free Radicals The Boot

Free radicals are nasty; they move throughout your body and damage it terribly. They're the by-products of all the neutralizing and detoxifying work that your lungs, liver, kidneys, and digestive system are doing. Therefore, the more crap you eat, the more load you place onto these organs, and the more nasty free radicals they produce. It is like you're handing your enemies a road map to your house.

So how do you diminish these suckers and their harmful effect?

You follow all the Simple tips throughout this book, you stop treating your body like a garbage disposal, and begin to take in more powerful antioxidants, which *surprise, surprise* are found most readily in raw, organic plant foods.

So ... Can A Healthy pH Help You Lose Weight? Yes!

That's because instead of eating processed foods that overload your body and deplete energy, an alkaline-friendly diet feeds your body whole, natural foods, for the best energy, digestion, and metabolism. Studies also show that a diet heavy in acid-forming foods promotes production of the stress hormone, cortisol, which in turn promotes the accumulation of abdominal fat. In other words, pay attention to the pH scale and not your bathroom scale and your body will reward you back!

It's so common for us to blame our extra stubborn pounds, particularly those around our waist-lines, on too many sweets and carbs, and while that may hold some truth for many individuals, it's not always the main culprit. I can pretty much guarantee that where there is extra weight, there is an imbalanced pH and fluctuating hormones.

Cortisol is enemy number one. High levels are linked to abdominal fat storage, memory loss, increased appetite, increased cravings, and lower muscle mass, bone density ... and even libido. And you're not exempt even if you are thin. Research suggests slender women suffering from chronic stress and high cortisol have more belly fat than people with normal stress levels, even those who carry more weight on their frames naturally.

So what can you do?

First, take things slowly. Read, read, and re-read certain portions of this book or the whole thing again, so that you begin to have a better understanding of acid vs. alkaline foods. Second, begin to understand that lower levels of cortisol are directly related to lower levels of stress.

Try deep belly breathing techniques, yoga and meditation, writing in a journal, and always getting a good night's sleep aiming to be in bed no later than 10:30 p.m. to 11:00 p.m.

Eat a high protein breakfast within one hour of waking and never go longer than three to four hours without eating a meal or snack.

If your stress levels are high, try using the herbal supplement, Relora, which helps to lower cortisol and establish healthy sleep patterns.

One of the best ways I've found to get on the right track, both personally and with my nutrition clients and yoga students, is by starting the day with a smoothie. It is a one-stop shop for all your dietary, pH, and hormone balancing needs. Here is an example of what you may put into your smoothie. Keep in mind that once you start moving a little deeper into whole foods and greens, you can start to make these smoothies more intense; however, for many in the beginning, this is a great place to start. The recipe below offers a great source of protein, calcium, magnesium, potassium, fibre, essential fatty acids, greens, and iron.

1 cup of almond, hemp, or brown rice milk
1 scoop of Vegan + protein powder by Genuine Health
½ banana and ½ cup frozen blueberries
1–2 tbsp either organic flax oil or ground flaxseed
Large handful of organic spinach, kale, or collards OR
    serving of a complete greens powder like spirulina
    or Greens + O (free of wheat and grasses)
1 tsp cinnamon
Blend all ingredients for 60 to 90 seconds and enjoy!

Each week, I teach ten to twelve classes, plus do my own strength training, swim, bike, and run workouts, and this type of smoothie kicks off at least six out of seven days, keeping my tank charged and my body feeling amazing!

CHAPTER 5

GETTING STARTED

5.1 Toss It! Burn It! Buy It!

Before you get excited and start into your new meal plan, you need to, TOSS THE JUNK and CHUCK THE CRAP!

Now is the perfect time to get rid of all the junk food that is currently in your house. Foods high in saturated fats and hydrogenated oils, sodium, sugar, and white flour should be thrown out first (e.g., cookies, ice cream, chips, pastries, candy, processed meats, soda, high-sodium frozen foods or soups, etc.). You know them. You think you love them. You also know THEY are the problem. Throw them away, and don't let anyone give you more.

Don't be nice. Don't take a bite. If people in your life are persistent and are begging you to join their "stay unhealthy and keep the crap party", you say: "Thanks but my ass and I have had a chat and we both feel it's in my pant's, my buttons', my bum-cheeks', my self-esteem's, and my sex life's best interest if I pass."

Then promptly give yourself a high-five and say congrats
Self!

You are now officially taking this program seriously!

Toss It. Burn It!

Pop, diet pop, flavour crystals, flavoured water, sports drinks,
diet or lite juice, sucralose, or all chemical and un-natural
artificial sweeteners.

Everything **white**: white bread, white pasta, white rice,
white flour, white sugar, and white table salt.

All **sugars** and foods containing sugars: cookies, puddings,
gelatin, candy, ice cream, etc.

Dairy. It's filling you with phlegm. It's giving you zits and
the shits. Let it go! No cow's milk or cheese. Be careful with
your ingredients, as many often say whey protein or casein
added, which are dairy by-products. Don't freak out—you
will be having cheese, but it will be goat cheese and your
milk will come from alternative choices.

Gluten. Begin to cut down on starches and pre-packaged
convenience foods that contain too much gluten.

Reduce your **meat** intake down to two times per week for
red meat, two times per week for chicken or fish, have zero
pork, ribs, chicken wings, etc., and make sure what you do
choose is organic, or you at least know where it is from and
how it was raised.

5.2 Understanding Ingredients In Our "Food" & On Labels

When you start to become a conscientious shopper, two things
happen: you begin reading the labels of everything you touch

in the grocery store and you add about an hour to your shopping time. Once you have discovered all of the amazing healthier products that await you out there, future shopping trips will be much easier and faster. However, I do encourage you to reread the ingredients from time to time, even the ones that look the best. It has happened to me before where I've been using a product for a while and rave about my faith in it, and then sometime later I will take a peek at the ingredients and they've changed! You have to stay on top of things.

The thing with ingredients is this: the longer the list, the more likelihood of the item containing poor quality ingredients. Try choosing products with shorter lists. Also note that the ingredients are in order of greatest quantity first, so if you see corn syrup solids listed near the top of five different types of sugar, e.g., molasses, sugar, barley malt, fructose, etc., you know this product is FULL of belly-busting sugar.

Artificial Colours

FD&C (Food, drug & cosmetic colours) are artificial colours used on food and in cosmetic and body care products. They can produce nasty effects in our behaviour and mood, and are extremely influential in your children's attitudes and ability to concentrate.

The main concern with these colourings is that they are typically derived from a source of coal tar. These have shown in numerous studies to cause cancer in animals as well as major allergic reactions. They are found in processed foods such as candies, cereals, children's snack foods, flavoured crackers, rice cakes, chips, hot dogs, condiments, icing, pop, etc.

- FD&C blue no. 1
- FD&C blue no. 2
- FD&C citrus red no. 2
- FD&C green no. 3
- FD&C red no. 2
- FD&C red no. 3
- FD&C violet no. 1
- FD&C yellow no. 5
- FD&C yellow no. 6
- FD&C yellow no. 7

Artificial Flavours

MSG (monosodium glutamate) is probably the most commonly seen and known of this group and rightfully so. Its side effects can include chest pains, headaches, nausea, numbness, inability to focus and concentrate, and memory loss. You need to be more aware than simply looking for MSG; it also has "sister" ingredients that can create the same or similar results.

These include: hydrolyzed vegetable protein, hydrolyzed plant protein, vegetable protein extract, yeast extract, glutamate, glutamic acid, sodium caseinate, textured protein, soy protein isolates, barley malt, calcium caseinate, and malt extract.

For a full listing of the many artificial flavours, visit http://www.cspinet.org/reports/chemcuisine.htm[6]

5.3 **The Dirty Dirts & The Clean Squad: Organics 101**

How many dirties do you know?

Part of teaching people how to eat healthy and stay on budget is helping them understand about the Dirty Dozen and The Clean Fifteen[7].

This fantastic resource will help you navigate your way through the grocery store as a more conscious and educated shopper. Yes, we would all love to buy everything organic, but for many of us, it just isn't possible. Fortunately, not all of your produce needs to be organic. When you are choosing conventionally grown fruits and veggies, use a good wash like Nature Clean Fruit and Veggie Soak; it's like a bath for your produce!

This year they have added two extra foods due to new findings. So I guess you can now refer to the Dirty Dozen as the Filthy Fourteen.

The Dirty Dozen

- Apples—91% of apples sampled were found to contain pesticides
- Nectarines
- Celery
- Peaches
- Strawberries

- Imported grapes
- Cucumbers
- Spinach
- Blueberries
- Lettuce
- Potatoes
- Bell peppers

The two NEWLY added are:

- Kale/Greens

- Green beans

Clean Fifteen:

• Onions	• Sweet peas	• Watermelons
• Avocados	• Kiwis	• Broccoli
• Pineapples	• Cabbages	• Cauliflower
• Mangos	• Eggplants	• Tomatoes
• Asparagus	• Papayas	• Sweet potatoes

A little something to think about as you do your shopping for the day!

5.4 Fats: The Necessary, The Nasty & The Oh No You Didn't!

Breaking News! Fat will not make you fat!

Say what? 'Tis true my friends, IF you consume the right types, quantities, and balance of fats, they will only work for you, not against you. We all need a Fat Facts 101 lesson to pull us out of the fat-fearing, fat-free craze that has riddled us for decades. Ever since we started eliminating fats we have increased our processed starchy carb intake, increased our chemical and artificial sweetener intake and chosen fake food like margarine, unhealthy, prepared commercial oils in spray form, whose name should really be, "I can't believe you never expire and never grow fur!" That's unbelievable. Wow! You must be so healthy for me.

Consumption of the foods listed above isn't the only thing that has increased; your weight, your pant size, your bra size (or perhaps your bro size for the men reading), may have grown too.

In order to achieve your ideal body weight, have energy, shiny hair, glowing skin, healthy cells, finger nails, and regular bowels, you need healthy fats.

There are different types of fat out there; what I need you to focus on is increasing your healthy essential fatty acids (EFA).

Your EFA Are Going To Help Your Body By:

- Helping the absorption and transporting of nutrients in your body
- Reducing inflammation throughout your body
- Increasing your metabolism
- Increasing your immune system
- Helping with hormone production and balance
- Lubricating your joints
- Supporting proper nervous system functioning and keeping the brain healthy

Great sources of your EFA are:
Sardines; wild salmon; flaxseeds; raw nuts and seeds such as walnuts, almonds, pecans, pumpkin and sunflower seeds; chia seeds; hemp seeds; salba seeds; and avocados. Even your dark leafy greens provide an excellent source, as well as many of your ancient and whole grains.

Change Up Your Oils

One of the easiest ways to liven up the taste of your food and make it healthier too is by adding some good quality organic, cold-pressed oils to your world!

Extra virgin olive oil, hemp oil, flax oil, avocado oil, macadamia nut and coconut oil, walnut oil, sesame oil, and

Udo's Oil (a blend of healthy oils) are fabulous additions to your kitchen. These are great for making salad dressings or drizzling over your prepared vegetable dishes. Never cook with these oils as they are very heat-sensitive. For cooking at low heats you can use olive oil; for higher heats, choose grapeseed, coconut, and sesame oil.

To decrease your overall oil use, try water sautéing or steaming your veggies first and then drizzle with oil once cooked.

Be sure to buy oils packed in dark bottles and store them in dark, cool places, as they can oxidize and go rancid quickly if they are exposed to sunlight and direct heat.

The Nasty & The "Oh No You Didn't!"

- High fat cuts of red meat
- Ribs, bacon, pork, and ham
- Commercially-baked pastries, cookies, doughnuts, muffins, cakes
- Packaged snack foods (crackers, microwave popcorn, chips)
- Margarine
- Vegetable shortening
- Fried foods (French fries, fried chicken, chicken nuggets, breaded fish)
- Chocolate bars and desserts

When it comes to eating unhealthy saturated and trans fats, there is one thing you need to remember before your lips hit the food and your teeth begin to chew.

Eating Hydrogenated Trans Fats = Having A Butt That Resembles A Golf Ball

A.k.a. cellulite and dimple central!

Not what we are trying to achieve here! For some of you, you may never be able to fully banish the bumpy appearance on your thighs and behind, BUT you can always improve from where you are now. It's four parts: 1) what you are eating, 2) how you are moving, 3) how you are sleeping and managing stress, and 4) how you are supplementing.

Once you have read the entire *Simplicity Project*, refer regularly to your Simplicity Project "On My Way To Feeling Awesome" checklist in Chapter 10, as a reminder of the daily and lifelong tips and steps you can be taking in your quest to Simply live your best life.

5.5 Your Simplicity Grocery List

PROTEIN

Beef (grass fed, organic)
Chicken/Turkey (organic)
Edamame beans
Eggs (free range, organic)
Goat cheese
Greek yogurt (organic)
Hummus
Kefir (similar to yogurt)
Organic beans (pinto, black, chickpeas, kidney, navy, etc.)
Scallops
Shrimp

Simplicity Bars,
   Elevate Me, Nature Bars
Spirulina and/or Chlorella
Tofu (2 x/month, max., organic)
Tuna (1 x/week max.)
Vegan protein powder (VegaOne, or Genuine Health Proteins+)
Wild salmon (canned, water-packed)
Wild fish (cod, bass, haddock, halibut, mackerel, perch, pollack, snapper, sole, trout)

VEGETABLES

Asparagus
Beets and root vegetables
Broccoli
Brussel sprouts and snap peas
Cabbages
Cauliflower
Celery
Cucumber
Eggplant
Green beans and peas

Kale, spinach, collards, chard,
    dandelion, bok choy
Lettuces
Mushrooms
Onions/scallions, leeks
Peppers (red, green, orange)
Rhubarb
Seed sprouts of all kinds
Sweet potatoes and yams
Zucchini

WHOLE GRAINS

Amaranth
Barley
Brown rice
Kamut

Millet
Oatmeal
Quinoa
Spelt

FRUITS

Apples
Bananas
Blackberries and strawberries
Blueberries and raspberries
Cherries
Grapefruit

Kiwis, pomegranates and mangos
Lemons and limes
Oranges
Peaches, pears and plums
Tomatoes
Watermelon

NUTS AND SEEDS

Almonds
Brazil nuts
Chia or Salba seeds
Flaxseeds

Pecans
Pumpkin seeds
Sunflower seeds
Walnuts and raw cashews

BREADS

Stonemill breads or Silver Hills
Ezekiel bread

BEANS AND LEGUMES

Black beans
Chickpeas
Kidney beans

Lentils
Split peas
White navy beans

BREAKFAST CEREALS

Ezekiel sprouted cereals
Large rolled oats (not instant)

Nature's Path cereals
7-grain hot cereal

PASTA

Brown rice pasta
Kamut or spelt

Quinoa pasta
TruRoots Quinoa Amaranth
    Brown Rice Noodles

SOUPS

Lentil
Organic vegetable broth

Vegetable and/or bean based

FATS AND OILS

Avocado (half is one serving)
Cold pressed organic flaxseed,
    sunflower, olive oil and
    grapeseed

Organic coconut oil (best for
    med-high heat)

CONDIMENTS AND SPICES

Apple cider vinegar (organic)
Balsamic vinegar
Braggs
Carob or cocoa powder
Dijon mustard (unsweetened)
Garlic

Herbs (all)
Real flavour extracts
Salsa (unsweetened)
Sea salt
Spices (all)
Tamari

DAIRY ALTERNATIVES

Almond milk (Earth's Own)
Brown rice milk (Earth's Own)

Coconut, hemp, oat, quinoa
Flax milk

SWEETENERS

Blackstrap molasses	Maple syrup
Coconut sugar	Organic sugar
Honey	Stevia

DAIRY

Goat cheese	Kefir (similar to Yoghurt)
Greek Yoghurt (organic)	

5.6 Your Kitchen: Organization + Equipment = Simplicity

You can be armed with the most amazing book, delicious meal plans, and best intentions; however, if your kitchen looks like a bomb went off in every corner, cupboard, and drawer, preparing fresh healthy meals will feel like a bigger chore than it's worth.

You need to have a place and space for everything, and have it all visually accessible so that you are not searching. If organization is not your strength, then you need to enlist the help of a friend or family member who has a penchant for this type of thing. Think about groupings: e.g., all your baking pieces, glass mixing bowls, measuring utensils, etc. in a cupboard; all your cutting boards, mandolin, spiralizers, slap-chop, baking sheets, oven mitts, and pot holders in another section, etc. For items such as your blender and/or juicer, keep them VISIBLE on the counter so that you use them!

These are some of the basics you should consider having in your kitchen so that you are well prepared:

Blender — my fave choices would be: The Magic Bullet for single servings, quick, and on the go; or the Vitamix, perhaps the Cadillac of all blenders, a hefty price tag, but soooo worth it!

Juicer — if you are a juicing virgin then starting off with a simple, less expensive one like the Jack LaLanne, Hamilton Beach, or Breville are good choices. If you are experienced and want to trade up, then I highly recommend the Omega 4000 or 8003.

Knives — Ideally, having a few options on hand is always good: a paring knife, a good chopping knife (chef's knife), serrated bread knife and a smaller serrated knife for slicing softer items.

Scissors — have one or two good pairs on hand for cutting, slicing and chopping herbs.

Cutting boards — one large wooden cutting board, or two or three boards of various sizes. Before you use them, treat them with a light coating of olive oil to seal the wood.

Peeler

Garlic press

Lemon juice extractor

Box grater

Spiralizer — a small appliance that creates long, fine, noodle-like strands from vegetables to make grain free "pasta" and add a sense of pretty and ingenuity to dishes.

Measuring cups and measuring spoons — have a combination of dry and wet measuring options.

Glass mixing bowls — have an assortment of sizes.

Steamer basket — I prefer a basket over a steamer machine because the basket fits easily into any pot and is a cinch to clean.

Stainless steel or cast iron pots and pans — avoid using non-stick pots and pans as they scratch easily allowing for the aging, chemical coating to flake off into your food. Plus when heated at or above medium to high heats they give off carcinogenic fumes that have been shown to lead to cancer, dementia and Alzheimer's, among other horrible issues.

Colander/strainers — a few different sizes are good to have.

Nut/milk bag — for making your own nut and grain-based milks.

Smaller fine mesh strainer

Spatulas, wooden spoons, ladle, tongs, whisk, slotted spoons, can opener, pizza slicer, and ice cream scoop are also necessities to have on hand.

Good quality, high-end food processor

Immersion blender

Coffee grinder — good for finely grinding seeds and spices.

Ceramic, glass (and only non-stick pans if you can't find otherwise) for baking, e.g., cake pans, cupcake/muffin pans, loaf pans, Bundt pans, and pie plates.

Mason jars — to store EVERYTHING!

The MOST important thing to have in your kitchen is MUSIC! This is a must. You need to have your mojo, food-love-makin' music on to take you on a journey with your food and meal prepping. Make it an experience and create memories!

5.7 Be Prepared & Budget Wisely

Every positive and successful outcome begins with a plan!

You need to strategize your way through meal planning and your grocery list if you are going to achieve your goals.

The first thing I recommend to my clients, once they have their meal plans, is to not go shopping. That's right, do not go shopping.

You need to take time to absorb what you are looking at, what you need to get, what you already have and more importantly, what you have that you need to TOSS and/or BURN. Plus you need to get your kitchen organized and ready, just waiting for all the new yummy food that will be coming its way.

Yes, eating a mostly organic, raw, whole foods-based diet can be more expensive—or not—depending on how you look at it. Have you actually ever sat down with all your receipts from grocery shopping, drive-thru-take-out, coffee shops, food trucks, vending machines, and other quick on-the-go places to see what you truly spend in one week? If the answer is NO, then for the next week I challenge you to do just this; EVERY single cent you spend, EVERY purchase you make, ask for a receipt. When you get home put your receipts into a Mason jar or basket; at the end of the week tally up what you have spent and notice WHERE your money has gone.

Then, prepare your grocery list for a week's worth of meal and snack inspirations from *The Simplicity Project* and do the same thing. BUT take the challenge a step further; pay extra attention when you are keeping your food journal to how you are feeling in your healthier, cleaner, more simplified week. Most of you will find that you have either spent less than when you were eating crappy, or you may have spent a small amount more but feel 100 percent better.

Small trade-off if you ask me. ☺

The other side of spending a little more now on healthier, nutrient-dense food is that you will spend less later on sick days, children's sick days, cough and cold medication, prescription drugs, fewer dental bills, and a lot less time waiting around at the doctor's office and walk-in clinic.

You need to set a food budget; you need to know how much you can afford to spend on your food, and how much food you really need. Walking around the grocery store grabbing whatever looks good or is on sale, without a plan of what to do with it, is a budget disaster waiting to happen. And don't even step into the grocery store if you are hungry. If you haven't had a chance to eat before shopping, head straight to the natural health section and buy yourself a healthy bar to eat while you shop. This way, you will be satisfied and have an action plan, a.k.a. your grocery list in hand, so that you can move through the store like you are on a mission. Then get the heck outta there so you can begin cooking!

Some Simple Ways To Cut Down On Your Grocery Bill:

Sit down with your family and create a weekly meal plan. Each family member can choose one healthy meal for the week and Mom or Dad gets to choose the rest. When everyone feels like they have been heard and had a vote for their meal of choice, they might be more likely to go along with the plan.

Once you have done your meal plan, create your grocery list based on this.

Now take a look through the grocery store flyers and price match so that you not only cut down on your bill, but your time running from store to store.

Commit to one large shopping for the week and one return visit to the grocery store for a re-stock of produce.

Get creative to cut down on waste. So many people I know purchase a whack of greens and veggies, and then don't know what to do with them, so they let them rot and then throw them out. Instead, try adding them to soups, stews, chili, ratatouille, casseroles, pasta sauce, or juice them. Or, you can freeze certain veggies that you can chop smaller or puree and fit into ice cube trays for later use.

For fruits, try juicing them, freezing for smoothies, or blending with a little water or almond, hemp, or coconut milk and making into healthy popsicles.

Make zero waste a policy in your household!

Start shopping at your local Farmer's Market and local farms or community-supported agriculture centre. You will be amazed at what you can get for your money and it's a fantastic way to learn more about food, how it's being grown and where it is coming from. To find great local farms and markets around you, try browsing the web or asking people with shiny hair and glowing complexions.

Grow your own garden! Herbs, tomatoes, cucumbers, lettuce, and zucchini are some of the easiest to get going. You can also purchase the amazing indoor, year-round Juice Plus Tower Garden[8], which offers you an abundance of growing possibilities for a very reasonable investment.

Buy in bulk. Big companies like Costco Wholesale are bringing in more organic, raw, wild, and fresh food every week; use them to stock up on main staples.

When choosing your produce; your fruits and vegetables, be sure to know your Dirty Dozen. They are the most harmful and highly sprayed/treated pieces of produce. You can shop based on the guidelines found at the Environmental Working Group website[9].

Don't overwhelm yourself anymore than you have to. Remember that this is a process. My journey and healthy process has been one that has been unfolding for the last eighteen years and continues to change and evolve all the time. The goal is to begin somewhere. One step at a time. Do the best you can and if you make a less than awesome choice—big deal! You are human, welcome to the club. Lick your lips and enjoy your meal; you sure as heck are not going back in there after it, so stop wading in the guilt pool. You have the chance to choose better and chew better at the next meal, so all is good! Also don't break the bank trying to become healthier; slowly make these changes and watch the new you become more and more alive with time.

CHAPTER 6

GETTING EXCITED FOR WHAT'S ON THE MENU

6.1 The Beverage Bar: Kick-Up Your Water Without Igniting Your Calories

I need you to start drinking more water now! Drinking at least eight to ten, eight ounce glasses or two to three litres daily, will help to keep your body hydrated and energized, the bowels moving regularly, your skin glowing, and toxins moving through and out of your body. Water is like fuel to your body, so stay properly hydrated. Don't wait until you're thirsty.

To help kick up the flavour of your water try some of these techniques:

Mint Water — ice water with fresh, torn mint

Lemon Water — ice water with lemon wedges

Lime Water — ice water with lime wedges

Basil Lemon Water — ice water with fresh lemon & basil

Fun Water — ice water with juice filled ice cubes

Grape Water — ice water with frozen grapes

Recovery Water — add one package of Emergen C powdered vitamin C

Cucumber Water — ice water with cucumber slices

Citrus Water — water with a splash of grapefruit or orange juice

Fruit Water — add fresh strawberries, blueberries, or pineapple to water

Green Clean Water — add five to ten drops of chlorophyll

Cold Brew Iced Tea Packages — add one

Blood Sugar Balancing Water — if you tend to be on the hypoglycemic side and have bouts of low blood sugar, especially during exercise, try adding a sweeter juice like apple, grape or mango to your water with a 50/50 split between the two.

Coconut Water — Nature's number one electrolyte balancing drink, providing you on average, with between 600 and 800 mg of potassium and up to 10 percent of your recommended daily allowance of magnesium; you can't go wrong with this drink.

Vitamin Water — is a once per week **TREAT** at 120 calories per serving. It may taste good but is it really worth it? Who is kidding whom here; this is **NOT** water, this is juice. Water is clear, has no flavour and comes from a Tap ... try it, your liver will luv ya!

After all, one glass of wine is 120 calories ... I don't know about you, but I would rather drink my water calorie and chemical-free, and ENJOY my vino fully and completely!

My Yogi Buns Are Freezin'! What Can I Drink To Warm Them Up?

I am not a coffee hater; however, there is a big difference between having a "cup o' joe" each day and a vase-sized-wine-glass-named litre of coffee each day! One to two cups of organic, naturally decaffeinated is best, but if you must have the caffeine make sure it too is organic when possible. There is such a vast array of delicious, aromatic, and soothing herbal teas out there now; the sky is the limit in choosing one. Use organic bagged tea or organic loose tea, which tends to have much richer flavour that also lasts longer!

Best Herbal Teas for Energy — Green Tea, Ginseng, Chai, and Rosehip

Best Herbal Tea for Digestion — Peppermint, Fennel, and Ginger

Best Herbal Teas for a Good Night's Sleep — Chamomile, Sleepy Time, and Lemon Balm

Best Detoxifying Start to the Day — Warm water, fresh lemon juice, touch of honey

6.2 Sassed Up Juices

Carrot/Apple Juice
6 carrots
2 apples

Bromelain Special
Pineapple (skin & all)
unscrew top and throw away

Liver Mover
2–3 carrots
½ beet

Orange or Grapefruit
3 oranges (peeled)
or 1 grapefruit (peeled)

Evening Regulator
2 apples
1 pear

Holiday Cocktail
2 apples
1 large bunch of grapes
1 slice lemon with peel

Rejuvenator
1 handful of parsley
3 carrots
2 celery stalks
2 cloves of garlic

Fresh
1 stalk celery
1 carrot
2 apples

Energy Shake
1 handful of parsley
6 carrots

Cantaloupe Juice
cut into strips and juice
(rind and all)

AAA Juice
6 carrots
1 apple
2 stalks of celery
½ handful of wheatgrass
½ handful of parsley
½ beet

Digestive Special
1 handful of spinach
6 carrots

Body Cleanser
4 carrots
½ cucumber
1 beet

Potassium Broth
1 handful of spinach
1 handful of parsley
2 stalks of celery
4-6 carrots

Passion Cocktail
4 strawberries
1 large chunk pineapple
1 bunch black grapes

Watermelon Juice
cut into strips and juice
(rind and all)

Sunshine Cocktail
2 apples
4-6 strawberries

Digestive Cocktail
¼ lemon with peel
½ grapefruit (peeled)
2 oranges

Morning Tonic

1 apple

1 grapefruit (peeled)

Alkaline Special

¼ head cabbage (red or green)

3 stalks of celery

6.3 Simplicious Smoothies

Adding in one scoop of hemp, rice, vegan, or 100 percent whey based protein powder is optional in each recipe. Some of my favourite brands are Vega One and Genuine Health Vegans + Protein. Other good whole foods protein sources include: Greek yogurt, raw nuts and seeds, spirulina, raw cacao, ground uncooked oats, and nut butters.

Vanilla Banana-Berry Smoothie

¾ cup vanilla almond milk

Small banana

½ cup frozen mixed berries

¼ cup orange juice

1 tbsp flax oil

Banana Cocoa Smoothie

1 banana

½ cup silken tofu or yogurt

½ cup almond milk

2 tbsp unsweetened cocoa powder

1 tbsp honey

Slice banana and freeze until firm. Blend tofu, milk, cocoa and honey in a blender until smooth. Add banana slices and continue to puree until smooth.

Coconut Milk Smoothie

1 small banana
½ pear
Handful organic baby spinach
1 tbsp organic flax oil plus 2 ice cubes
1 cup So Good Organic Coconut Milk
1 scoop Vegan + Vanilla Protein Powder

Chocolate Monkey Smoothie

1 scoop hemp, vegan or 100% whey protein powder
1 cup chocolate almond milk
2 tsp all-natural peanut or almond butter
1 banana plus 1–2 ice cubes

Fruit Creamsicle

1 banana
½ cup orange juice
½ cup milk alternative
½ cup frozen berries
1 tbsp maple syrup
3 ice cubes

Pure Energy

1½ cup liquid (I used 1 cup coconut water,
    ½ cup almond milk)
1 cup spinach
1 small banana
3 dates
2 tbsp raw cacao powder or unsweetened cocoa powder
1 tbsp flax oil
1 tbsp maca powder
1 tsp spirulina (optional)
Ice to your liking

Blend in a high powered blender and feel the energy.

Purple Haze

½ banana
½ cup frozen blueberries
1 handful spinach
½ cup almond milk
¼ cup pomegranate juice
½ cup Greek vanilla yogurt
1 tbsp ground flaxseed
1–2 ice cubes

Summer Sunshine

1 cup organic orange juice
15 strawberries
1 banana
2 tsp ground flaxseed

Place all ingredients into blender and blend until creamy.

Enzyme Boost

½ cup diced pineapple
½ cup frozen mango
1 cup rice milk
1 tbsp honey
1 tsp vanilla extract
Squeeze of lime juice

Almond Yogurt Smoothie

½ cup rice milk
¼ cup water
4 tbsp vanilla yogurt
10 almonds
1 banana
4 dates or 1 tbsp maple syrup
1 tbsp flax oil
Ice

Pina Colada

1 cup rice or almond milk (vanilla is nice in this)
½ cup pineapple coconut juice
1 banana
½ cup fresh pineapple
1 tbsp lime juice

Green Power Smoothie

½ cup milk
½ cup apple juice
Large handful of spinach or kale
4 dates
1 banana
1 scoop protein powder
1–2 ice cubes

6.4 Safe & Sinful Sweeteners

Safe Sugar Substitutes

According to Sharecare[10], a website that sources experts to answer your health questions, Dr. Mehmet Oz said the following when it comes to sugar:

"The average person consumes 150 pounds of sugar per year—compared to just 7.5 pounds consumed on average in the year 1700. That's 20 times as much! When typical slightly overweight people eat sugar, they on average store 5% as ready energy to use later, metabolize 60% and store a whopping 35% as fat that can be converted to energy later.

Interestingly, 50% of the sugar we consume today comes from high-fructose corn syrup in fat-free foods like salad dressings and regular soft drinks.

Pretty gross when you hear about it in those terms. While the obvious message here should be to drastically cut down on your sugar consumption, the reality is that some sugar is still going to make its way into your food and onto your plate, with the final destination being your body ... the temple!"

Here are some general recommendations to replace one cup of refined, white sugar:

- **Agave Nectar** (¾ cup). Reduce liquid in recipe by ¼ cup for every cup of agave used.

- **Brown Rice Syrup, Barley Malt or Honey** (1¼ cups). Reduce liquid in recipe by ¼ cup.

- **Maple Syrup** (1 cup). Reduce liquid in recipe by ¼ cup for every cup of maple syrup used.

- **Molasses** (½ cup). Reduce liquid in recipe by ½ cup. Molasses is very high in certain minerals such as iron, calcium, copper, magnesium, potassium, and manganese.

- **Sucanat** (1 cup).

- **Stevia** (⅛ tsp whole leaf powder = 1 tsp sugar; ⅜ tsp = 1 tbsp sugar; 2 tbsp = 1 cup sugar. Amounts differ if you are using liquid or white powder form. See the product label.) Stevia is an extract from the stevia plant and is much sweeter than white sugar so much less is needed.

Sinful Sweeteners

I am floored at the amount of people and children I see around me every day with a can of diet pop in their hand, sugar-free yogurt, or latte, believing that this is their healthier choice.

We have become so diet-obsessed that unless we actually see the word "diet", we are sceptical as to whether or not there are any health benefits to the "food". We have, sadly, allowed our education about food to come from thirty-second commercials as opposed to real knowledge and information.

The Worst Of The Worst

In November, 2011, an article was published on the mercola. com website, entitled *Aspartame is, by Far, the Most Dangerous Substance on the Market that is Added to Foods.*[11] Here are some excerpts:

> "Aspartame is the technical name for the brand names NutraSweet, Equal, Spoonful, and Equal-Measure. It was discovered by accident in 1965 when James Schlatter, a chemist of G.D. Searle Company, was testing an anti-ulcer drug ....
>
> ... Aspartame accounts for over 75 percent of the adverse reactions to food additives reported to the FDA. Many of these reactions are very serious including seizures and death. A few of the 90 different documented symptoms listed in the report as being caused by aspartame include: Headaches/migraines, dizziness, seizures, nausea, numbness, muscle spasms, weight gain, rashes, depression, fatigue, irritability, tachycardia, insomnia, vision problems, hearing loss, heart palpitations, breathing difficulties, anxiety attacks, slurred speech, loss of taste, tinnitus, vertigo, memory loss, and joint pain... .
>
> ... Aspartame is made up of three chemicals: aspartic acid, phenylalanine, and methanol. The book *Prescription for Nutritional Healing*, by James and Phyllis Balch, lists aspartame under the category of 'chemical poison.'..."

... *How Aspartate (And Glutamate) Cause Damage*

Aspartate and glutamate act as neurotransmitters in the brain by facilitating the transmission of information from neuron to neuron. Too much aspartate or glutamate in the brain kills certain neurons by allowing the influx of too much calcium into the cells. This influx triggers excessive amounts of free radicals, which kill the cells. The neural cell damage that can be caused by excessive aspartate and glutamate is why they are referred to as 'excitotoxins.' They 'excite' or stimulate the neural cells to death....

... The excess glutamate and aspartate slowly begin to destroy neurons. The large majority (75 percent or more) of neural cells in a particular area of the brain are killed before any clinical symptoms of a chronic illness are noticed. A few of the many chronic illnesses that have been shown to be contributed to by long-term exposure to excitatory amino acid damage include:

- Multiple sclerosis (MS)
- ALS
- Memory loss
- Hormonal problems
- Hearing loss
- Epilepsy
- Alzheimer's disease
- Parkinson's disease
- Hypoglycemia
- Brain lesions
- Neuroendocrine disorders

Splenda (Sucralose)

Splenda is not natural; it is a chlorinated artificial sweetener. This is a topic and debate that could go on forever. Much like the above-explained effects of Aspartame and its equal partners, Splenda has many adverse side effects, and when a company like Whole Foods makes a statement such as this below, I sit up and listen.

"Sucralose is an artificial substance that is not found in nature, like aspartame and hydrogenated fats. Although supporters of sucralose claim that it is unable to be metabolized, up to 35% is absorbed by the body with a lifespan up to 23 hours."[12]

6.5 Simplistic Bars & Bites

A great combination of some homemade bars and bites and also some handy, healthy store bought ones too!

Almond Bites

2½ cups rolled oats
½ cup raw pumpkin seeds
½ cup raisins
2 tbsp raw sunflower seeds
1 tsp cinnamon
½ cup almond butter
⅓ cup plus 1 tbsp honey
2 tbsp barley malt syrup
1 tsp vanilla extract
(optional 1–2 tbsp spirulina powder)

Grind ½ cup oats and ¼ cup pumpkin seeds in food processor until powdery. Transfer to a medium bowl, set aside.

Combine remaining 2 cups oats, remaining ¼ cup pumpkin seeds, raisins, sunflower seeds, and cinnamon in a large bowl. Stir in almond butter, honey, barley malt syrup and vanilla until soft dough forms. If you are using spirulina, add in now as you are mixing.

Moisten hands, and roll dough into 1" balls. Coat balls in oat-pumpkin seed powder. Place in freezer 20 minutes to set, then serve or store in the fridge.

Crispy Brown Rice Squares

½ cup brown rice syrup
3 tbsp nut or seed butter
¼ cup chopped, dried fruit (apricots, cranberries, etc.)
½ cup almonds, coarsely chopped
1 tsp vanilla
3 cups crispy brown rice cereal

Combine first two ingredients in a large saucepan. Simmer over medium to low heat. Add dried fruit of choice and almonds and simmer 5 minutes more; remove from heat.

Stir in vanilla and cereal. Mix thoroughly (moistening your hands a bit helps). Firmly press mixture into a lightly oiled 8" x 8" square pan. Using a sharp knife, make light indentations to denote 2" squares (this will expedite in cutting later).

Refrigerate about 30 minutes. Cut into 16, 2" squares.

Energy Bites

½ whole-grain spelt flour
⅛ tsp baking soda
⅛ tsp baking powder
¼ tsp sea salt
½ tsp cinnamon
⅓ cup Sucanat

1½ cups toasted almonds, chopped
½ cup dried cranberries
12 Medjool dates (approximately 1 cup chopped dates)
1 cup organic dried apricots, cut into bite size pieces
1 flax egg (1 tbsp ground flax + 3 tbsp water)
1 tbsp almond or rice milk
1 tsp pure vanilla extract

Preheat oven to 325°F. Line an 8"x 8", or 9"x 9" square pan with parchment paper across both sides for easy lifting. In a small bowl mix together the flax egg and set aside.

Chop and toast the almonds for 8 to 9 minutes at 325°F. Remove from oven and set aside. Toasting the nuts really brings out the flavour so you don't want to skip this step.

In a large bowl, whisk together the flour, baking soda, sugar, baking powder, cinnamon, and salt. Stir in the almonds and dried fruit. Make sure the nuts and dried fruit are all coated with the flour mixture.

Mix the vanilla into the flax egg once it has thickened, after about 10 minutes.

Add the flax egg mixture and the 1 tbsp almond milk to the fruit and nut mixture and mix well. Spread into the pan, pressing with fingers to even it out. I have used a pastry roller too.

Bake for 33 to 35 minutes at 325°F or until golden in colour. Remove from pan and allow to cool on wire rack for 10 minutes. Now transfer back into the pan and place in freezer to set for 10 minutes. Remove from pan once again and allow to cool for about 10 minutes. Now slice the bites up with a sharp knife.

Makes 16 to 20 bites depending on how large you make them.

Homemade Almond Butter Brownie Lara-ish Bars

1 tbsp almond butter
1 tsp vanilla extract
1 cup walnuts
1⅓ cups dates
1 tbsp ground flax seed
A handful of chocolate chips

Place the ingredients into your food processor and let that blend for a couple minutes, or until everything is nicely chopped and turned into a dough. Once it's all mixed up, take a handful of dough and form it into bars. You then can wrap them up and place them in the fridge to harden or enjoy one now!

Store Bought Bars That I Love!

Check out your local health food store for some of these great bars. I keep a bin in the pantry at home filled with great bar choices that my husband, kids and I can help ourselves to when we're in a hurry. I also have a few stashed in my various purses and bags just in case!

- The Simply Bar
- The Nature Bar
- Vega Bars
- Greens +
- Elevate Me
- The Kind Bar
- Bumble Bar
- Luna Bars, in moderation, as they contain soy

6.6 Simply Irrestible Nibbles

Everyone needs a little treat once in a while, and although I approve of small indulgences, it doesn't mean that I'm saying you should go all out and *overindulge*. Choose wisely and choose as healthfully as you can. Eating something delicious doesn't have to ruin all your hard work or give you a food hangover. Keep it real—real food, real enjoyment!

Chocolate Dipped Apricots

24 whole organic dried apricots
6 oz organic dark chocolate
12 almonds, finely chopped

Prepare a baking sheet by lining it with parchment paper. Place the chopped almonds in a small bowl. Melt the chocolate in a medium bowl.

One by one start coating the apricots, first with chocolate and then with almonds. Place them on the prepared baking sheet, and repeat for the remaining apricots.

Put in the refrigerator for approximately 10 minutes. A chocolately fibre treat to indulge and keep you going strong.

Mango Mousse

1 mango
½ tbsp of coconut oil
3 tbsp of agave nectar
½ tsp chia seeds

Melt coconut oil on very low heat. Combine all ingredients in a standard blender on high until creamy and smooth. Cool in the fridge and enjoy!

Chocolate Orange Brownies

4–6 servings
3½ cups soaked & dried walnuts
½ cup raw cacao powder
8 Medjool dates, pitted
Zest of ¼ orange
Pinch of celtic sea salt

Soak your organic walnuts overnight, or for at least 6 hours. Drain the water and rinse the walnuts thoroughly. Lay the walnuts to dry overnight. Combine all the ingredients in a food processor, except Medjool dates. Process until fine. Add dates and process until combined. After the brownie dough has come together, form it into desired shapes and finish by sprinkling some chopped walnuts on top for decoration.

Avocado Chocolate Pudding

4 ripe avocados
1 cup raw cacao powder
½ cup maple syrup
5 Medjool dates, pitted
½ cup coconut oil
¼ tsp whole vanilla bean powder or scrapings of
   1 vanilla bean

Blend all ingredients in a high speed blender, constantly using the tamper since the consistency will be very thick. Once the pudding has reached a silky texture, scoop into a bowl and decorate with fresh fruit.

Banana Spelt Vegan Chocolate Cake With Fresh Berry Coulis

A fresh vegan twist on my Mom's cake that I grew up enjoying every year for my birthday. Thanks Mom ☺ ☺ ☺

Pre-heat your oven to 350°F and bake for 45 to 50 minutes.

Sift Together:

3 oz cocoa

½ tbsp baking soda

1 tsp baking powder

½ tsp and a bit of sea salt

2 cups of spelt flour

1 cup organic sugar

Add wet ingredients:

½ cup plus ⅓ cup organic sunflower oil

1 cup either almond, rice or coconut milk

5 well mashed or blended bananas

Mix all ingredients well and pour into your greased Bundt pan.

Place into the oven on the centre rack and bake for 40 minutes. Insert a wooden toothpick into the centre of the cake, and if it comes out clean you are good to go. If not, put back into the oven for another 5 minutes.

Once done, allow to cool for 10 minutes. Place a flat plate over the top, flip upside down and give a firm smack on the bottom to release the cake.

You can choose to serve plain (delicious) with fresh fruit or you can take some fresh berries and blend them with a little raw honey, maple syrup or agave nectar until you achieve your desired consistency and sweetness for a super easy berry coule.

6.7 Sensible Eating Out & Eating Well

Eating fresh home-cooked meals isn't always possible, and is not a requirement seven days per week in order to feel and look your best. I have included a list of healthier eat out/take out options for you and your family to enjoy.

North American Cuisine

- Grilled fish, chicken, or shrimp on lush green salad
- Steamed vegetables
- Seared tuna
- Vegetable based soups
- Grilled vegetable wrap

Sub Shop Or Deli

- Always choose whole grain, 100 percent rye, sprouted bread, gluten-free or 100 percent whole wheat
- Load on the vegetables
- Grilled chicken or nitrate free turkey
- Vegetables, avocado, sprouts, and humus or tzatziki
- Salad

Japanese

- Sashimi
- Sushi
- Chicken or salmon teriyaki, sauce on the side with no white rice and extra vegetables
- Salads, edamame or miso

Greek

- Salads
- Fresh calamari
- Chicken skewers and steamed or grilled vegetables
- Whole-wheat pita with humus

Italian

- Salad
- Shrimp cocktail
- Grilled shrimp, fish or chicken
- Whole wheat or gluten free pasta primavera

Mexican

- Salad with grilled fish or chicken
- Soft tacos or burritos with grilled fish, chicken, or extra veggies
- 100 percent corn nachos with fresh salsa or fresh guacamole
- Skip the excessive cheese and sour cream

Coffee Shop

- Whole grain bun or bread with vegetables or either light cream cheese or sliced cheddar cheese
- Salad and/or soup
- Yogurt and granola parfait

- Egg with fruit
- If available (Starbucks) protein kit with fresh fruit, cheese, flax crackers, and humus
- Fresh fruit
- Smoothies
- Healthy bars such as Larabar, The Kind Bar, or The Simply Bar
- If you are surrounded by healthy eat-out options, such as great vegetarian or vegan restaurants, you're pretty much safe in your choices.

6.8 Your Simplicity Project 7-Day Sample Meal Plan

	Day 1	Day 2	Day 3	Day 4	Day 5	Day 6	Day 7
BEGIN EVERY MORNING	Warm water fresh lemon tsp raw honey	Warm water fresh lemon tsp raw honey	Warm water fresh lemon tsp raw honey	Warm water fresh lemon tsp raw honey	Warm water fresh lemon tsp raw honey	Warm water fresh lemon tsp raw honey	Warm water fresh lemon tsp raw honey
B-FAST	Raw Cacao, Coconut, Banana Smoothie	Green Power Smoothie (recipe under sensational smoothies chapter 6)	Enzyme Boost Smoothie (recipe under sensational smoothies chapter 6)	Red Velvet Smoothie	Vanilla Banana Berry Smoothie (recipe under sensational smoothies chapter 6)	2 organic egg omelet w/spinach & red peppers ½ Ezekiel English Muffin tsp Earth Balance Coconut Butter or Real butter	1 cup Mesa Sunrise Nature's Path cereal SUPER TOPPERS tbsp of each raw walnuts, raisins, raw sunflower seeds Almond milk

SNACK (optional if more then 3 hours has passed)	1 cup chopped kiwi and pineapple; 12 raw cashews; Jenn's Dressing	Energy Bite	¼ cup Nature's Path Hemp Granola; 4 Tbsp Organic Greek Yogurt	Navel Orange	The Kind Bar	Organic Pink Lady Apple; Tbsp almond butter	¼ cup raw almonds, cashews, walnuts, & tbsp dark chocolate chips
LUNCH	1 cup Quinoa salad veggies, ½ avocado cubed, tbsp goat cheese, 2 tbsp each pumpkin & sunflower seeds; Jenn's Dressing	Large mixed greens salad loads of veggies, ½ avocado cubed, goat feta, raw pecans and hemp seeds; Jenn's Dressing	1 cup Black Bean Avocado salad; 8 Mary's Brown Rice Crackers	1 cup Imagine Organics Butternut Squash Soup; Tuna 'salad' made with fresh chopped veggies and served over salad greens	Small baby greens salad; Amy's Brand Gluten Free Bean Burrito	1 cup Kamut Rotini Pasta salad topped with veggies and served with protein rich Green Goddess dressing	Veggie and humus platter, Guacamole and organic tortillas, Think along the lines of mini-appies

SNACK	20 Fresh Snap Peas 2 tbsp humus	Veggie pate rolled into a giant lettuce or collard leaf	4 domino pieces goat Cheese 8 Mary's Brown rice Crackers	Apple 20 raw almonds	20 tortillas & ½ avocado mashed with lime juice S&P	Smoothie Option (see Sensational Smoothies)	Healthy Bar option (see Simplistic Bars & Bites)
DINNER	Warm Portobello, Roasted Red Pepper and Feta Salad	Home made Black Bean and Rice Burritos Visit jennpike.wordpress.com for recipe	Wild Salmon Grilled veggies Massive Salad	Pear Walnut Goat Cheese Salad Poppy Seed dressing 3 oz. lean beef	Wild Haddock Green Bean and Beet Toss ½ baked Sweet Potato	Imagine Organic Cashew Carrot Soup Goat cheese, roasted red pepper, basil Panini's	Kale, Red Cabbage, Beet, Carrot Salad Avocado dressing ½ cup short grain brown rice

For all the recipes noted above, please refer to Chapter 6, sections 6.3, 6.5, and 6.9.

6.9 More Simplicity Project Recipes

Smoothies

Red Velvet Smoothie

1 cup chocolate almond milk
1 cup frozen raspberries plus handful organic spinach
½ fresh banana *or* ¼ fresh avocado
1 scoop vanilla Vegans + protein powder
2 tbsp flax oil

Blend 60 to 90 seconds

Raw Cacao, Coconut, Banana Smoothie

1 banana pre-frozen into slices
1 cup coconut milk
2 tbsp raw cacao nibs
1 tbsp honey
2 tbsp flax oil

Blend milk, cacao and honey in a blender until smooth. Add banana slices and continue to puree until smooth.

Veggie Paté

(A loving gift from my friend and mentor, Caroline Dupont, author of *Enlightened Eating*)

1 cup sunflower seeds, soaked 4 to 6 hours
Small carrot
½ cup broccoli, chopped

½ cup cilantro or parsley
1 clove garlic
1 tbsp lemon juice
1 tbsp miso paste

Process seeds, carrots, broccoli, cilantro or parsley and garlic clove. Add remaining ingredients and mix well by hand.

Enjoy this on whole grain crackers, or stuffed into a wrap or collards

Protein Rich Green Goddess Dressing

1 clove garlic, minced
1 small avocado
½ cup tahini
6 tbsp water
3 tbsp apple cider vinegar
2 tbsp fresh lemon juice, to taste
¼ cup extra virgin olive oil
½ cup fresh basil leaves
½ cup fresh parsley
1 leek
1 tsp sea salt, or to taste
1 tsp tarragon
½ tsp maple syrup

Add garlic clove to food processor and process until finely chopped.

Add in the water, oil, avocado, tahini, herbs & leek. Process until smooth. Now add in the lemon juice and apple cider vinegar. Finally add in the salt to taste. Taste and adjust seasonings to your liking. Store in an air-tight container or jar in the fridge. Will keep for 5 days.

Poppy Seed Dressing

½ cup raw cashews, soaked for 30 minutes,
   rinsed in cold water
¾ cup cold-pressed extra virgin olive oil
¼ cup filtered water
3 tbsp freshly squeezed lemon juice
2 tbsp honey
½ teaspoon sea salt
2 tbsp poppy seeds

In a blender, combine cashews, oil, water, lemon juice, honey, and salt. Blend at high speed until smooth.

Transfer to a container and stir in poppy seeds. Serve immediately or cover and refrigerate for up to 5 days.

Jenn's Dressing

⅓ cup olive oil
2 tbsp balsamic vinegar
1 tbsp fresh orange juice
1 tbsp maple syrup
1 tsp Dijon mustard
Salt and pepper to taste
Whisk together the ingredients.
Makes ½ cup

Store in an air-tight container or jar in the fridge. Will keep for 5 days.

Black Bean Avocado Salad

1 organic red pepper, diced
3 stalks of celery, chopped
1 can black beans, rinsed
1 cup organic corn niblets

½ cup cilantro, chopped
1 avocado, diced
2 tbsp olive oil
2 tbsp lemon juice
1 tbsp Dijon

Mix oil, lemon juice, and Dijon in the bottom of a large bowl. Add pepper, celery, beans, corn, cilantro, and avocado and stir to mix. Serve at room temperature.

Warm Portobello Roasted Red Pepper And Feta Salad

1 large bin of organic, pre-washed mixed salad greens
1 cup thinly sliced, roasted red peppers
2 large, washed and thinly sliced Portobello mushrooms
¼–½ cup feta (Macedonia is creamy and is great with this)
2 small garlic cloves, minced
1 green onion, finely chopped
2 tbsp olive oil
2 tbsp balsamic vinegar
Salt and pepper to taste

Heat a medium to large pan over medium heat and add tbsp of olive oil, add the minced garlic and green onions and let simmer. Add in mushrooms and sauté until mushrooms are starting to brown. Add in roasted red peppers, additional tbsp of olive oil, balsamic vinegar, salt and pepper. Begin to crumble in feta. Add the greens right into the pan and combine lightly with tongs.

Pear Walnut And Goat Cheese Salad
With Poppy Seed Dressing

1 bin of pre-washed organic greens or
   a combination of greens

1 yellow pepper, julienned
12 cherry tomatoes, halved
1 pear, thinly sliced
½ cup walnuts
Herbed goat cheese, enough to crumble over top

Create a bed of greens and top with yellow peppers, tomatoes and pear.

In a saucepan, add a little olive oil, and over low-medium heat, pan-roast walnuts until brown, drizzle with honey, toss, and top over salad.

Add goat cheese and enjoy!

Beet Infused Green Beans And Hemp

4 cups green beans, stemmed and halved
2 cups grated beets
¼ cup Jenn's salad dressing
2 tbsp hemp seeds

Lightly steam green beans for 3 to 4 minutes.

Transfer to a medium bowl and toss with beets, dressing and seeds.

Kale, Red Cabbage, Beet And Carrot Salad

1 head of kale, stem removed and chopped finely
1 leek
1 cup grated red cabbage
1 beet and 1 carrot, each grated
½ cup dried cranberries

In a large bowl toss together kale, red cabbage, beets, carrot, leeks and cranberries.

Serve with Jenn's Dressing poured into a blender with 1 avocado plus 2 tbsp water

CHAPTER 7

CREATING THE BODY YOU WANT FOR LIFE

7.1 Step Off The Scale & Into Your Closet: Understand Your Body Composition

You are more than a number on the scale, and judging yourself or allowing that number staring back at you in the morning to affect your mood, your energy, and perhaps the rest of your day is no way to live your life. As of right now, stop making your weight your goal. Instead, I want you to focus on how you are feeling; let's get you eating better and more balanced, sleeping more, having more sex, on a solid supplement schedule, and actually wanting to exercise. The simple fact is, if you're not feeling great and you have no energy, you won't want to work out, plan meals, or cook healthier food for yourself and your family.

Your primary goal to change your body should be to

increase the amount of lean muscle tissue you have and decrease the amount of fat tissue you have. This is what we refer to as your body fat percentage—your fat to muscle ratio. Muscle is the key to long, lean, sculpted arms and legs, flatter tummies and firmer derrieres. The majority of the thin, super models you are drooling over and wishing you could look like, probably have very high body fat percentages; this is not your goal. You might also be familiar with the Body Mass Index (BMI) chart. This shows the healthy or not so healthy balance between your height and your weight based on your age; in my experience not always a great tool—it either states the obvious or tells us nothing.

It would be ideal for you to book an appointment with a qualified personal trainer or strength and conditioning specialist, to have your body fat test done and your measurements taken, so that you really know where you are starting from, and that you have the information that truly matters.

Your body fat matters because it will have a massive impact on your overall health. Extra fat on our bodies means more work for our vital organs to breathe, function, and communicate effectively with each other. Plus, extra fat will contribute to wicked cravings, extra yeast, and nasty digestion.

Did you know that we are all born with a pre-set amount of fat cells?

It's true and you can never, ever, no matter what you do (unless of course you suck it out), lose fat cells. However, you can gain additional fat cells by living a lifestyle of inactivity, processed food, high stress, poor sleep, little joy, and poor supplementation. You can gorge or fill your current fat cells until they become so full they divide; one fat cell becomes two fat cells.

So now it has just become twice as hard to lose weight and, more importantly, to maintain the loss because as I mentioned earlier, you can gain new fat cells but you can never lose them. Two can quickly become four, six, and so on. There is no quick fix, there is no magic solution ... it simply does not exist. You must work hard, be consistent, create an action plan for success and have a way to stay accountable to your goals—to yourself!

The next time you think about the scale, move towards your closet instead. You need to pay more attention to how your clothes are fitting. If there is stuff coming out over the top (in front and behind), if you have to perform squats before you can wear your jeans, or if the seams are screaming for help, it doesn't matter what your scale says; you know you need to make changes now!

The healthy range of body fat for women between the ages of twenty and fifty, is 17 to 25 percent, but optimal is 20 percent.

7.2 Losing Fat & Building Lean, Long, Strong Muscles From Head To Toe

Cardio is the best way to lose weight. WRONG! This is one of the most common exercise myths that I have heard over and over in my fifteen years in this industry.

Day after day, I would walk into the gym I worked at for over ten years and see the same people on the cardio machines doing the same "fat-burning" pre-set program and shake my head. I'm talking about the treadmill users who "walked" the same route every day, happily watching the big screen TVs, and those on the recumbent bikes leisurely pedalling while reading and yawning. Regardless of which cardio machine they chose, the one thing they ALL had in common was that their bodies NEVER changed, EVER!

Now don't get me wrong; these people were at the gym and they were exercising, but there is a big difference between being there in presence, and BEING PRESENT. The individuals who would show up and merely go through the paces might lose a few pounds in the beginning, but their shape, muscle tone and their metabolic systems never made a shift significant enough to give them the desired look, feel, or health they were looking for.

The More Muscle You Have On Your Body, The More Fat You Will Burn—Period.

You will even be burning fat while you sleep and for sixteen to thirty-six hours post-exercise, depending on the type and intensity of exercise, current state of health, and foods consumed before and after; this is a phenomenon called EPOC, Exercise Post Oxygen Consumption.

Plus, muscle burns fat and fat fuels fat. Yuppers, the more fat you have, the more fat you store. All of your hormonal signals are being sent and received from your fat, so your fat, in fact, actually controls how much more fat you store. You really do need to stop this cycle and take control of your fat cells in order to have any success in losing weight and keeping it off.

I'm not saying that my balanced approach of yoga, pilates, and sculpted will be IT for you; we are all built differently and it takes time, trial, and experience to figure out what works for you. This will not happen over one month. But, if after three or four months you are not seeing results and you are putting in the necessary effort, it's time to try something else. If you are not sure what else to try, email me; I am FULL of suggestions.

7.3 Get Strong Not Scrawny: Your Twice Weekly Dose of Sculpting

I can't tell you how many clients I have worked with over the years who have convinced themselves that if they just push harder with their exercise, their thyroid will magically become balanced and they will lose weight. The unfortunate reality is, and many studies have proven this, that long periods of strenuous activity actually stress out and lower your thyroid hormones. Hmmm, well now this creates a problem since your thyroid hormones are what fire up your metabolism. The other issue is that these types of exercise sessions not only lower your thyroid but they increase your cortisol and once again lead you back to no sleep, poor recovery and an ever-expanding waistline ... not to mention one ticked off version of you.

As a result, I advocate twenty to thirty minutes of intense, circuit-style weight training sessions that work a number of muscle groups, instead of the traditional forty-five to sixty minutes. While the amount of time you train is important, so too are the types of exercises that you choose. I am a huge fan of functional strength training, as well as offering progressive overload training to your accessory/stabilizing muscles. However, when you are short on time you need a combination of both to create optimal results.

Choose compound exercises that train two or more muscle groups simultaneously, to increase your body's metabolic response and the amount of muscle fibres you are recruiting, plus the calories you are burning. You will never meet a more intelligent or effective machine than your own body, so start using it as your main source of resistance. For weighted exercises, free weights or kettle bells are the way to go. You need to train your muscles unilaterally, so that each muscle is being trained effectively and is equally challenged to avoid creating muscular imbalances in your body. Also choose a few exercises that help you isolate stabilizing muscles, specifically those of the abdominals, glutes, inner and outer thighs, and your hips.

You should perform roughly eight to ten exercises per workout, moving quickly from one to the next with very little rest between sets. Do as many as you can with good form. Why do you stop at repetition twelve or fifteen when you can keep going? If you are not uncomfortable you are not changing! (Remember, I said uncomfortable, not in pain.)

Workout A

- Squats into a standing shoulder press
- Reverse lunges into single leg bent row
- Step-ups into bicep curls
- Push-ups into side plank
- Kneeling side leg lift
- Medicine or Pilates ball side-to-side oblique twist
- For an added bonus try adding thirty- to sixty-second bursts of cardio such as running on the spot, skipping, jump squats, or jump lunges to amp up your training.

Workout B

- Push-ups into kneeling donkey kicks
- Plank with one arm row
- Plié squats into lateral shoulder raise

- Shoulder press with standing leg extension
- Forward lunges with bicep curls
- Squats into standing tricep overhead extension
- Oblique crossovers until you cannot crossover one more time

Stay tuned Summer 2013 for your **exclusive link** to *The Simplicity Project—Your Best Body Yet* videos offering the best of Yoga, Pilates and Functional Strength Training!

7.4 Shake Your Butt! Calm Down Cardio Queen. This Is Short, Sweet & Sweaty

Many believe the best cardio for fat burning is forty-five to sixty minutes at a moderate pace. Others swear by long, endurance style cardio sessions. The truth is neither endurance training, nor setting the treadmill or elliptical to the "fat-burning" zone, is the way to your desired body. You don't need to spend hours in the gym or even one hour for that matter. With the right combination of exercises and high intensity intervals with short recovery periods, you will be well on your way to the body you've always wanted.

There are many studies that have shown when you decrease the time you spend training, but increase the intensity through interval training or circuits, you increase the effectiveness and your results. One study in Australia from the University of New South Wales in Sydney[13] showed that after only twenty minutes of interval-based training, individuals had a higher rate of spiking fat-burning hormones than another group that performed forty minutes of cardio at a moderate, continuous pace.

Choose twenty to thirty minutes, maximum two days per week. Here are a few sample workouts that are home-based or can be done outdoors:

Option #1: Power Walk With Jogging Intervals

- Warm up with five minutes of moderate paced walking, pumping your arms for extra action.
- Power walk for four minutes and jog for one minute, for a five-minute set.
- Repeat this five-minute set three to five times.
- Cool down with three to five minutes of moderately paced walking.

Option #2: Jogging With Running Intervals

- Warm up with five minutes of power walking.
- Jog for three minutes and run for two minutes.
- Repeat for three to five sets.
- Cool down with three minutes or jogging and two minutes of walking.

Option #3: Stairs, Skating & Suicides

- This one is to be done at home; grab your runners and you are good to go!
- Warm up five minutes by running on the spot, knee ups, jumping jacks, skipping, and knee-ups in that order for one minute each.
- Run the stairs for one minute

- Power skate from side to side one minute
- Run on the spot with heel-butt kicks one minute
- Suicides — running from one spot to about six to ten feet away, touch the ground with your hand and run back to the other side and hit the ground for one minute
- All outs — open your feet wider than hip width, squat down slightly, arms in front, now run it on the spot as fast as you can.
- Repeat this entire set three times
- Cool down with one minute of stairs, some side-to-side shuffling, walking on the spot and some good old breathing!

7.5 Strike A Pose: Unroll Your Yoga Mat & Discover A Journey Like No Other

Today's practice sheds some light on the importance, the serenity, and the strength that yoga has to offer you. The most amazing part about yoga is that there is no moment, in any posture, that your whole body is not being challenged and fine-tuned, when your mind is not engaged, your breath is not integrated, and your whole soul-self isn't vibrating with potential.

Please visit my YouTube channel link below for your exclusive look at some of my 20-, 30- and 40-minute calorie torching power vinyasa yoga sequences as well as videos filled with nutrition, skin care, recipes, strength training, pilates and so much more! http://www.youtube.com/user/JennPikes? feature-mhee[14].

7.6 The Busy Person's Guide To Meditation ... A Work In Progress

Believe me; I have had a love/hate battle with meditation for years. Initially my attitude was that I didn't have time for it. And what was the point? I could be doing so many other more "important" things. It wasn't until I stopped putting so much pressure on myself for *how* the meditation had to happen that it just started to happen. I began to sneak in moments of quiet, with my eyes closed and focused breath. When I could, I chose meditation through movement, walks, yoga—and especially with music, which is very important to me; it feeds my soul and my spirit.

I also stopped worrying about what I was thinking and simply quieted my mind. Instead I chose to notice what I noticed and to remember something very important...

Energy Flows Where Attention Goes

Try this beginner's guide to meditation:

Sit or lay down in a comfortable position and in comfortable clothing. You may want/need blankets, pillows, bolsters or blocks to support you.

Close your eyes and begin to focus on moving your breath through your entire body. Breathe into your belly, your heart, your throat, and your head.

Notice and put equal amounts of energy and effort into both your inhale and your exhale. If it takes you five to six seconds to breathe in, then take five to six seconds to breathe out.

Now move your breath into your shoulders, down your arms, into your wrists, your palms and your fingers. Smile.

Breathe down into your lower back, hips, front and back of your thighs, your knees, calves, shins, ankles, feet, and toes. Smile.

Take five full breaths through your ENTIRE body. Inhale through your nose and exhale through your nose.

Draw in one slow, long breath through your nose and a deep exhale through your mouth.

Softly begin to wiggle your fingers and toes; let your arms and legs move into a hug, gently rocking from side to side.

Roll to your right side for three to five breaths, slowly rising when you are ready.

Take a deep breath in, palms together at your heart. Softly exhale and bow.

Namaste.

CHAPTER 8

SIMPLIFYING SUPPLEMENTS— AN INTEGRAL PART OF YOUR PROJECT!

I hope by this point in the book you have come to recognize the importance of your nutrients, vitamins, minerals, fibre, etc. coming from your healthy, best food choices first. That being said, there are some very good arguments and reasons to support why adding in a few super nourishing, super powerful supplements are in your body's best interest. First, most of us do not get the recommended daily amount of fresh fruits and vegetables, or enough fibre and essential fatty acids. Second, unfortunately the soil used to grow our food and the food that feeds animals is nutrient-deprived and depleted.

I try not to bog down my clients' systems with too many pills and powders, and instead focus on a very balanced plan of supplements that I refer to as "lifers" and "for right now".

Your "lifers" are: probiotics, vitamins C and D, super foods and protein powders, B vitamins, essential fatty acids, and digestive enzymes.

Your "for right nows" are: anything particular to an acute issue we are dealing with or something hormone specific. These are the supplements in which you will probably need greater guidance from a qualified holistic nutritionist, naturopath, or classical homeopath.

Be sure of one thing: supplements are NOT to replace the food you actually need to consume. They are going to enhance or complement what you are already eating and practicing. You also want to be sure that the brand you are purchasing is of good quality. Please avoid the least expensive brands on the shelves, and those that are strictly in the pharmacy section. Choose your supplements from natural/health sections of your grocery stores, or head to a health-specific store that specializes in supplements. Better yet, make an appointment with a qualified holistic nutritionist to determine what is best for you and your body.

8.1　Give Your Gut a Boost: Probiotics

Did you know that about 70 percent of your immune system is located in your gut?

That's right! Now don't you think keeping your pretty little belly healthy and full of good bacteria to fend off the bad "dudes" is kind of important?

I will answer this one for you—YES!

So how do we become unbalanced and unhealthy in our guts? There are many ways; but mainly, it is when we eat poorly, take medications (prescription or not), or undergo treatments like chemotherapy, that the majority (if not all) of our good bacteria guys will be wiped out. This is why I call probiotics "lifers". ☺

When you go into a health food store or health section of a grocery store, you will notice quite a few brand choices. Be sure to choose one that is vegetarian and enteric-coated. This coating will help to protect the bacteria inside the capsule until it leaves your stomach and all of its lovely acids, and enters into your small intestine. Choose a brand with bacterial counts into the billions (yes billions) and remember it must be kept in the fridge. There are a few brands that are shelf stable for when you travel and don't have the room to pack your fridge! ☺

Some of my favourite brands are:

- Genestra HMF Forte
- Biotics BioDoph 7
- Sisu
- Innovite
- Genuine Health Liveprobio + Omega 3

Another fabulous way to restore your gut and intestinal flora is to drink a cup of Kombucha daily. Made from sweetened tea that's been fermented by a symbiotic colony of bacteria and yeast (a SCOBY, a.k.a. "mother" because of its ability to reproduce, or "mushroom" because of its appearance), Kombucha is one of the most amazing elixirs for detoxification and immunity due to its extraordinarily antioxidant-rich content. It's also a known probiotic beverage, improving your digestion and fighting candida (harmful yeast) overgrowth.

8.2 Your B Squad

The B vitamins support the adrenal glands, which in turn help us to adapt and flow more gracefully with stressors of the day. When you are stressed, your B vitamins rush to respond and your body depletes them quite quickly, leaving you feeling tired and listless. Stressful anxiety is the number one threat to a woman's health and happiness.

Women with premenstrual syndrome (PMS), depression, low energy and under-active thyroid would be doing themselves, their families, and their friends a great favour by taking a complete vitamin B complex. B vitamins help your body to better access nutrients and energy in food. These vitamins need to be replaced daily because they are water soluble and easily washed out of your system (hence the florescent urine you will notice once you start taking Bs).

Some of my favourite B complex brands are Sisu B Stress, Biotics C Complex, and Genestra has a few good B products.

The one B vitamin you will need if you are becoming vegetarian or vegan is B12, and that is because it isn't found in plant food. Your body can't make it on its own so you will need to supplement. Sublingual or liquid are best so that they get absorbed right into the blood stream. Be sure that the one you choose contains B12 in the form of methyl-cobalamin—you absorb this best.

Good brands are Trophic, Biotics, Genestra, and Land Art.

8.3 Real True Vitamin C

Nothing irks me more than when I hear people, more specifically parents, say, "Of course my children are getting enough vitamin C; they have a glass of commercial orange drink each morning." *Oh dear* (imagine a sad face) is all I can think and I am usually left speechless and dumbfounded.

Vitamin C is found naturally highest in our adrenal glands (remember ... your body's SWAT response team to stress!), so it's no shocker that this vitamin is depleted daily and needed just as often. Vitamin C is a super powerful antioxidant that helps to fight off those nasty free radicals circulating your body. It is also an essential component to having a strong, balanced immune system and for collagen production in your skin, ligaments, and tendons. I strongly suggest taking a minimum of 2,000 mg daily; however, if you are under extra stress or beginning to feel under the weather I would up it to 6,000 to 8,000 mg daily. My preferred source of vitamin C is Emergen C. They are convenient, easy-to-use powdered packages, making them ideal for travel; plus they add a great flavour to your water for those of you who complain that water is boring ... sigh. I also love Emergen C because it contains bioflavonoids and some B vitamins, which enhance the use and activity of vitamin C in your body.

8.4 Sun-Shiney Vitamin D

Although we refer to vitamin D as a vitamin, it really functions more like a hormone, being produced in the body, helping to enhance your metabolic system, all cellular functions, and the integrity of your genes. Vitamins, by definition, are not produced by our bodies and must be obtained from dietary sources. One of the most common and serious deficiencies in the body in terms of vitamins is vitamin D, and this can have some very critical consequences. Low vitamin D levels in North America are now being linked to an increased risk and rate of diseases such as cancer, multiple sclerosis, osteoporosis, osteopenia, heart disease, infertility, rheumatoid arthritis, depression, SAD, ADD, ADHD, fibromyalgia, Alzheimer's, obesity, insulin resistance, and diabetes.

Some of the more common symptoms of low vitamin D are:

- Fatigue
- Muscle pain and weakness
- Muscle cramps
- Chronic pain
- Weight gain
- Restless sleep and/or insomnia
- Poor concentration and memory
- Headaches

Vitamin D is on top of many jobs within your body. It's literally everywhere. Most tissues and cells in your body have vitamin D receptors, which have the ability to interact with more than two thousand genes. The majority of us living in North America, unless we work outside and are exposed to the sun daily, are either deficient or in need of daily supplementing to ensure that we don't become deficient.

The best form of vitamin D is from the sun; it's made by your skin in response to the ultraviolet exposure. A mind-blowing fact is after only twenty minutes of pure exposure to the sun, it can produce 20,000 IU of vitamin D! I know, crazy eh?! Now, don't you think there is a reason your body produces so much of it, so quickly and naturally, when given the right circumstances?

By the right circumstances I mean you can't be slathered in sunscreen and get these benefits. Your skin needs to be bare. The interesting thing is that when you do go out for ONLY twenty minutes with no sunscreen, you don't burn, you tan slightly, a clear sign of positive vitamin D action happening. I highly recommend you test this for yourself.

I know, right now you just re-read what I wrote ... NO SUNSCREEN? What the heck is this girl talking about? For years now, we have all been *scared to death* to go outside in the sun without sunscreen because of the risks of skin cancer. However, in the last few years, the same doctors and dermatologists that said this, have now discovered that moderate exposure to sunlight helps the body produce the amount of vitamin D needed to keep our bones strong and our cells healthy, even protecting us against certain types of cancer, including skin cancer. What researchers are also discovering is that individuals who apply commercial, chemical-filled sunscreens (which work to completely block any of the sun's UV radiation from penetrating the skin, and allow the body to produce vitamin D,) often have a higher rate of skin and other types of cancers. This is because the chemicals and parabens, etc., are literally being baked into your skin— which, by the way, is your body's largest organ and number one digester of all things it comes in contact with. We will discuss more on this topic in Chapter 9.

You simply cannot get all of the required amounts from your food, because few foods naturally contain vitamin D. Some oily fish like wild salmon, mackerel, tuna, sardines, shitake mushrooms, and egg yolks are the best sources. There are also fortified foods that contain vitamin D, but you would have to consume copious amounts in order to get the recommended dosage. When supplementing, it is also important to get the adequate amount needed by your body to perform all vitamin D's daily tasks.

How much vitamin D you need really depends on the individual, but as a base, you should be taking a minimum of 2000 to 4000 IU daily in vitamin D3 form or vitamin D2 if you are vegan. If you feel like you are coming down with something, are under extra stress, or work an office job and never get outside, or if you have an auto-immune disease, cancer, heart disease, (plus any of the side effects I listed previously of not getting enough of this critical vitamin), then supplement with 5000 to 10000 IU daily for no more than three months. Then reduce down to 2000 to 4000 IU daily. Liquid and/or sublingual is best and easiest to absorb.

My number one choice for vitamin D is Biotics D Mulsion.

8.5   Cheers to Fat! Why Your Body Needs Fat To Lose Fat

Essential fatty acids are called that because they are ESSEN-TIAL to the overall health, cellular functioning and well-being of your entire body. However, you do not produce them, so you need and must obtain them solely from your diet and your supplements.

EFAs support and nourish your cardiovascular, reproductive, immune, and nervous systems. Your body *100 percent* needs EFAs to manufacture and repair cell membranes, enabling the cells to obtain optimum nutrition and expel harmful waste products. One of the major roles of EFAs in the body is their production of prostaglandins which help to maintain your heart rate, blood pressure and clotting. Prostaglandins are also necessary for healthy fertility and actual conception of a baby, plus they are vital in a strong immune system by encouraging your body to fight off infections.

Omega 3 fatty acids (linolenic acid) are used in the formation of cell walls, making them supple and flexible, and improving circulation and oxygen uptake with proper red blood cell flexibility and function. Ensuring you get enough of your Omega-3s is so important because they are quite literally involved in nearly every cellular process happening in your body. Everything from healthy hair, skin, digestion, vision, immunity and moisturizing you from the inside out to decreasing PMS and menopause symptoms, lowering your blood pressure and cholesterol. They are called ESSENTIAL for a reason!

Where Do You Find Omega 3 EFAs?

- Flaxseed — be sure to use a combination of whole (insoluble fibre but great to act as an internal exfoliator) and ground plus flax oil for optimal results
- Hemp oil, hemp hearts and heart seeds
- Raw walnuts, almonds, pecans and brazil nuts and their raw nut butters
- Pumpkin seeds, sunflower seeds, sesame seeds, chia seeds, savi seeds and Salba
- Avocados, olive oil, macadamia oil and coconut oil
- Salmon, tuna, sardines and anchovies

So why is all this Omega info so important to know about? Because without these wonderful Omegas your body simply cannot function to its full potential or abilities. Period.

Remember this one very important thing: you cannot and will not lose weight, maintain that weight loss, and lead a vibrant life, if the sum of all your life choices, including all dietary aspects, is not clean, vibrant and healthy. You know this is true. Just look around at all of the individuals (you might even be one of them) who can't lose any weight, or keep losing and then regaining over and over again.

Make sure that all your oils are kept in cool, dark places to prevent them from going rancid, and that all your raw nuts and seeds are kept in either the fridge or freezer for best freshness. Also, note that certain oils such as flax and hemp should be kept in the fridge; other healthy oils such as olive oil, grapeseed, sesame, coconut oil, etc. can be kept in the cupboard.

8.6 Protein Powders & Super Foods

Super Foods

Super foods are those that are ridiculously rich in phytonutrients (natural and unique plant properties that have disease-fighting powers). These amazing phytonutrients can reduce your risk of cancer, help to decrease inflammation, arthritis, digestive conditions, strengthen your immune system and boost your overall energy, vitality and well being. The top food sources are:

Blue Green Algae — Helps to improve mental focus, clarity and energy, regenerate cells and fight free radicals head on. It is also a major source of vitamins and minerals, which can assist in keeping your blood sugars balanced.

Spirulina — This algae is super high in protein and chlorophyll. It tastes nasty, but if you can get creative with it and add it to smoothies or take it in a tablet form, you will have one rockin' bod from it!

Chlorella — This superhero helps to balance pH levels and reduce acidity in your system. It's also very helpful in regulating the bowels, increasing your immunity, and binding to heavy metals and radiation.

Chlorophyll — If I had a dime for every time someone asked me, with a nasty look on their face, what was in my water, I would have a lot of dimes. ☺ I put chlorophyll in my water every day and have for the last twelve years. It is a liquid super food that is rich in iron, helps to purify your blood, your liver, deodorizes your breath and body from the inside out, and also helps to regulate the bowels.

Green Powders — I love Genuine Health's product, Greens + O. It's organic and free of grasses unlike their original formula, which for people who suffer from seasonal allergies was not so awesome. I use this product between my classes to keep acidity and free radicals down, and love how convenient it is to ensure I am getting my daily dose of awesome into my body!

Protein Powders — I'm a huge fan of protein powders because with the busy lifestyle I lead, I can completely understand how challenging it can be to get the necessary daily nutrients you need from your protein sources. I also do not eat red meat, pork, chicken, or drink milk or use cow cheese. I choose vegan or vegetarian-based protein powders that are made from either hemp, rice, pea, cranberry, alfalfa, spirulina or add in raw cacao and carob powders or raw nuts like cashews, almonds, and walnuts plus raw seeds like sunflower, hemp, chia, flax, and pumpkin.

Some of my favourite brands of powders are:

- Genuine Health Vegans + Protein Powder in vanilla
- VegaOne Protein Powder in chocolate
- Sun Warrior Protein Power is also good

The reason I choose vegetarian over dairy formulated whey-based powders is because I firmly believe the average individual is taking in WAY TOO MUCH DAIRY, leading to massive amounts of inflammation, congestion, the intake of too many hormones and antibiotics, etc. When I hear people say they are lactose intolerant, I cannot hold myself back ... WE ARE ALL LACTOSE INTOLERANT! WE'RE NOT COWS. ☺ ☺ ☺

It is estimated that some 70 to 90 percent of all ailments, disease, autoimmune disorders, allergies and a big chunk of cancers are greatly affected by the intake of cow's milk products.

8.7 Digestive Enzymes, Apple Cider Vinegar & Aloe Vera Juice

It really depends on the individual, but for most clients I see, there is usually some form of a digestive aid that I recommend to help the efficiency of their digestive system. It does not matter what issue you present to me. As a nutritionist, my main focus is to build you a solid digestive foundation through better food, better balance, and less stress from both external factors and internal treatment. If you have been eating an average diet for the majority of your life, if you have ever taken a course of antibiotics, had a stomach virus, battled any bowel issues, or if your stomach is where your stress centres its energy, than you need a digestive enzyme.

I take into consideration, through specific questions, the severity of your digestive issues. If they are mild I will most likely suggest taking apple cider vinegar, one to two tbsp before meals, to provide enough HCL (hydrochloric acid) in the stomach. For someone without a gallbladder, it is not a question of IF they should take a digestive enzyme; it is a MUST for the rest of their life. They need one with bile and pancreatin. When choosing the right digestive enzyme for you, make sure the supplement has at least three types of enzymes: protease to break down protein, lipase to break down fat, and amylase to break down carbohydrates. Plant-based enzymes are best and much easier on your system because they're similar to what your body is already producing, or trying to produce.

8.8 Hormone Specific

The Simplicity Project has been designed to open your eyes to vast layers of life that have been moving through your body and how everything is connected. There is truly no beginning or end and one area of stress in the body will undoubtedly lead to additional stress and symptoms throughout. When it comes to balancing out your hormones, your first and foremost goal should be to have a more solid understanding of where you are currently by completing your Hormonal Health Profile. Then begin eating in a more nurturing and supportive way, supplementing consistently, sleeping better, exercising five days per week, having more sex, using better skin care and body care products, spending more time journaling, writing, dancing, singing, reading ... whatever it is that brings more joy into your life.

Once you have begun to do all of these wonderful things, then we can begin to talk about *if* your hormones need supplemental rebalancing and what you need to add in or take out.

I would highly recommend booking an appointment with a naturopathic doctor to have full blood work, saliva testing, and signs/symptoms recorded and tested. This is, from both my experience and my knowledge, the best way to treat hormonal imbalances. Under a naturopath's guidance who can recommend bio-identical hormones, herbs, supplements, tinctures, etc., you will receive the most effective treatments possible.

A Final Note On Supplements

You really do get what you pay for when it comes to your supplements, so please do yourself, your gut, and your *sweet ass* liver, the courtesy of a little research and patience in this area until you find a great brand and get fantastic results.

The best way to educate yourself on top quality brands is to ask those who work in the holistic industry, or visit your local health food store.

CHAPTER 9

TREATING YOUR WHOLE BODY LIKE A GODDESS

9.1 Your Largest Organ Is Your Skin & It Eats ALL DAY LONG!

Now that you've made such an impact on your skin's appearance by eating healthier and living better, natural skin care products are the best way to finalize your commitment to yourself and your health and to get you glowing all over!

Did you know that women use an average of twelve to fourteen personal care products every day? Think about it: soap, face wash, toner, scrub, lotion, night cream, day cream, sunscreen, shaving cream, shampoo, conditioner, styling products, make-up, and deodorant. Wowza! Don't you think it makes sense then, to know more about the products and, better yet, the ingredients going onto and INTO your skin? Remember: your skin is your largest organ and eats, or more accurately, absorbs EVERYTHING it comes in contact with.

We all want beautiful, soft, clear, glowing skin, but what price are you willing to pay for it? I know numerous people in my life who have turned to laser, harsh microdermabrasion and chemical peels, all in the quest for great skin and a more youthful appearance, but they've had either minimal benefits or some negative side effects at the same huge cost. However, I also know many more people in my industry and my immediate circle of colleagues and friends, who use a more holistic, herbal and natural approach to their skin care, and have far better results at a fraction of the price.

Daily, we use these fabulous smelling, prettily packaged and sweetly marketed products that we think are safe; but the truth is that some of these products are NOT safe, and their manufacturers don't have to tell us. Since 1938—when the FDA granted self-regulation to the cosmetics industry— personal body and cosmetic products have been marketed without government approval of ingredients, regardless of what tests show. Most of the 25,000 chemicals used have not been tested for long-term toxic effects. On an average day, you might be exposed to over 200 different chemicals, many of which are suspected of causing cancer or manipulating your hormones. EPA tests conclude that ingredients in shampoos, dyes, and other personal care products may be playing havoc with hormones that control reproduction and development.[15]

The actual term is referred to as transdermic penetration, meaning that your products are either going right into your blood stream via the skin, or the skin is being affected by the product in some way. Is your head tilted to one side right now with a sketchy look of "yeah right" on your face? Well, if you don't believe that this is true, think about a few common products that are put directly onto the skin to affect the body: the patch for quitting smoking, the patch for mosquito repellent, cold and flu patches, birth control hormone patches, and hormone replacement patches. Convinced yet?

Here Is A List Of The Biggest Offenders In Terms Of Ingredients:

Parabens: Parabens are the most widely used preservatives in cosmetics. They are also used as fragrance ingredients, but consumers won't find that listed on the label. Fragrance recipes are considered trade secrets, so manufacturers are not required to disclose fragrance chemicals in the list of ingredients. Parabens easily penetrate the skin and are huge xenoestrogens; chemicals that mimic estrogen, the primary female sex hormone. They have been detected in human breast cancer tissues, suggesting an association between parabens in cosmetics and cancer.

Parabens may also interfere with male reproductive functions. In addition, studies indicate that methylparaben applied on the skin reacts with UVB (Ultraviolet B rays), leading to increased skin aging and DNA damage, another case for the increase we've seen with skin cancer since everyone has been slathering on chemical sunscreens.[16]

"Alcohol, Isopropyl (SD-40): a very drying and irritating solvent and dehydrator that strips your skin's moisture and natural immune barrier, making you more vulnerable to bacteria, molds and viruses. It is made from propylene, a petroleum derivative, and is found in many skin and hair products, fragrance, antibacterial hand washes, as well as shellac and antifreeze. It can act as a 'carrier' accelerating the penetration of other harmful chemicals into your skin. A Consumer's Dictionary of Cosmetic Ingredients says it may cause headaches, flushing, dizziness, mental depression, nausea, vomiting, narcosis, anesthesia, and coma.

DEA (diethanolamine), MEA (Monoethanolamine) & TEA (triethanolamine): hormone-disrupting chemicals that can form cancer-causing nitrates and nitrosamines ... Dr. Samuel Epstein (Professor of Environmental Health at the University of Illinois) says that repeated skin applications ... of DEA-based detergents resulted in a major increase in incidence of liver and kidney cancer. The FDA's John Bailey says this is especially important since 'the risk equation changes significantly for children.'"

It is important to note that these chemicals are restricted in Europe due to known carcinogenic effects.

"DMDM Hydantion & Urea (Imidazolidinyl): just two of many preservatives that often release formaldehyde which may cause joint pain, skin reactions, allergies, depression, headaches, chest pains, ear infections, chronic fatigue, dizziness, and loss of sleep. Exposure may also irritate the respiratory system, trigger heart palpitations or asthma, and aggravate coughs and colds ....

... FD&C Colour Pigments: synthetic colours made from coal tar, containing heavy metal salts that deposit toxins into the skin, causing skin sensitivity and irritation ... Animal studies have shown almost all of them to be carcinogenic." (cancer causing).

"Fragrances: Mostly synthetic ingredients can indicate the presence of up to four thousand separate ingredients, many toxic or carcinogenic. Symptoms reported to the FDA have included headaches, dizziness, allergic rashes, skin discolouration, violent coughing and vomiting, and skin irritation.

Clinical observation proves fragrances can affect the central nervous system, causing depression, hyperactivity, irritability, inability to cope, and other behavioural changes."

Think of how you feel instantly overwhelmed, needing to escape before you hurl, when you smell someone wearing way too much perfume or cologne.

A great alternative to these chemical fragrances is to use essential oils.

"Mineral Oil: petroleum by-product that coats the skin like plastic, clogging the pores. Interferes with skin's ability to eliminate toxins, promoting acne and other disorders. Slows down skin function and cell development, resulting in premature aging. Used in many products such as baby oil, which is 100% mineral oil!"

A great alterative: Use almond oil, jojoba oil, or evening primrose oil on your baby's skin and your own.

"Polyethylene Glycol (PEG): A ... carcinogenic petroleum ingredient that can alter and reduce the skin's natural moisture factor. This could increase the appearance of aging and leave you more vulnerable to bacteria. Used in cleansers to dissolve oil and grease. It adjusts the melting point and thickens products. Also used in caustic spray-on oven cleaners ....

... **Propylene Glycol (PG) and Butylene Glycol:** gaseous hydrocarbons, which in a liquid state act as 'surfactant' (wetting agents and solvents). They easily penetrate the skin and can weaken protein and cellular structure. Commonly used to make extracts from herbs. PG is strong enough to remove barnacles from boats! The EPA considers PG so toxic that it requires workers to wear protective gloves, clothing, and goggles and to dispose of any PG solutions by burying them in the ground. Because PG penetrates the skin so quickly, the EPA warns against skin contact to prevent consequences such as brain, liver, and kidney abnormalities. But there isn't even a warning label on products such as stick deodorants, where the concentration is greater than in most industrial applications....

... Sodium Lauryl Sulfate (SLS) & Sodium Laureth Sulfate (SLES): detergents and surfactants that pose serious health threats. Used in car washes, garage floor cleaners, and engine degreasers, and in 90% of personal-care products that foam. Animals exposed to SLS experience eye damage, depression, laboured breathing, diarrhoea, severe skin irritation, and even death. Young eyes may not develop properly if exposed to SLS because proteins are dissolved. SLS may also damage the skin's immune system by causing layers to separate and inflame. When combined with other chemicals, SLS can be transformed into nitrosamines, a potent class of carcinogens. Your body may retain the SLS for up to five days, during which time it may enter and maintain residual levels in the heart, liver, the lungs, and the brain....

... Triclosan: a synthetic 'antibacterial' ingredient—with a chemical structure similar to Agent Orange! The EPA registers it as a pesticide, giving it high scores as a risk to both human health and the environment. It is classified as a chlorophenol, a class of chemicals suspected of causing cancer in humans. Its manufacturing process may produce dioxin, a powerful hormone-disrupting chemical with toxic effects measured in the parts per trillion; that is only one drop in 300 Olympic-size swimming pools! It can temporarily deactivate sensory nerve endings, so contact with it often causes little or no pain. Internally, it can lead to cold sweats, circulatory collapse, and convulsions. Stored in body fat, it can accumulate to toxic levels, damaging the liver, kidneys and lungs and can cause paralysis, suppression of immune function, brain hemorrhages, and heart problems. Tufts University School of Medicine says that triclosan is capable of forcing the emergence of 'super bugs' that it cannot kill. Its widespread use in popular antibacterial cleaners, tooth pastes, and household products may have nightmare implications for our future."

The fake "natural" skin-care companies: There are also many so-called natural skin care companies that use these chemicals in their cosmetics as well. They knowingly deceive their customers by including a few token natural ingredients within their chemical concoctions. They then market these as natural skin care products. Some of the major players in this deception are your average and most popular brand name body care products.

9.2 Simplistic Skin Care

Face — You want to be gentle with the skin on your face and avoid harsh, abrasive washes and scrubs. Knowing your skin type is an important place to start; try visiting the cosmetic section of your local health food store for some help determining your skin type.

- Start your day off rinsing your skin with tepid water, not hot. Try to avoid cleansers first thing in the morning as you will strip your skin's natural moisture over time. Save your cleanser for the evening, after a day of wearing make-up, being exposed to environmental toxins, and sweating.

- Next, spray a natural toner over your face and gently press it into the skin with your fingertips. I love the toners from Dr. Hauschka, but you can also very easily make your own. Refer to the recipes below.

- If you are prone to blemishes apply your cream or gel (be sure it contains no more than 5% benzoyl peroxide) and try not to use it each day.

- Apply a water-based, natural, lightweight moisturizer to your skin. Choose something with either an organic form of sunscreen or one that has a coconut, borage, jojoba, or shea base for protection.

- For your make-up choose products that are in a base of vitamin E or olive oil and contain minerals such as zinc, which will also provide a natural source of sunscreen. I like Mineral Fusion, Zizu, Say Yes to Carrots, Jane Iredale and Dr. Hauschka.

- In the evening, use your gentle face wash and use almond oil on a cotton swab for your eye make-up remover.

- Spray your toner and apply a light coating of oil; either evening primrose, almond, jojoba, coconut, or shea or you can apply some nourishing aloe vera directly from your plant to your skin and be amazed when you wake in the morning to find no pimples, only glowing hydrated skin staring back at you from the mirror.

Body — Your body care should be very simplistic and truly a three-step process:

1. Alternate between daily dry brushing using a natural bristle brush, starting from your extremities and taking long sweeping motions up towards your core and heart centre; and on the alternate days use a natural, gentle scrub like the one I have provided for you below.

2. Wash your body with a natural soap such as oatmeal, emu oil, evening primrose oil, kelp, or cucumber. These soaps will also double as an excellent replacement for shaving cream.

3. Hydrate your skin while it is still damp from the shower with a rich oil like almond, jojoba, coconut, or shea. They will leave your skin so silky smooth and last the whole day without re-applying.

Try these three fabulous recipes to add to your new Simplicity Skincare Toolbox:

Hydrating Face Mask (great for dry or over-treated skin): Blend or mash half of a ripe avocado with a small bit of rice milk and honey. Apply a generous coating to your face and neck, cover your eyes with cucumbers, lay back, and practice the skill of chillin' for fifteen to twenty minutes. Rinse with warm water and voila! Gorgeously soft skin.

Simple Lavender Toner (great for oily, combination and acne prone skin): This toner is great for the face and for the whole body to add a nice fragrance instead of chemical body sprays.

Small spray bottle
1 tbsp lavender buds from your garden or maybe a friend's
1 cup witch hazel
6 drops of lavender essential oil

Combine all ingredients in a glass mason jar and store in a cool, dark place for two weeks to steep; you must shake it vigorously everyday. Once the two weeks are up, drain the liquid and store in your spray bottle. Use within six months and this may be left on your bathroom counter.

Coconut Vanilla Brown Sugar Body Scrub: This scrub is so amazing, I have given it as a gift to many great ladies in my life and keep a container in the shower at all times.

You will need a BPA-free plastic container (glass is good if you are leaving it on the counter, but if it goes in the shower do not use glass).

1¼ cups organic brown sugar
6–8 tbsp organic coconut oil
15–20 drops of either pure vanilla essential oil
   or organic food grade vanilla

In a bowl combine the sugar and coconut oil. Add the vanilla oil drop by drop, blending as you do. No refrigeration is needed. It must be used within six months but don't worry ... it won't last that long!

Use this in the shower one to two times weekly to exfoliate your skin. I find when I use this, my skin is so soft I don't even need to apply my oil after.

Some Additional Things To Consider For Your Skin Care "Tool Box"

- Bathe your skin in sunlight daily for ten to twenty minutes or when possible.
- Shower in lukewarm or cool water morning and evening. Finish off showers with the water as cold as possible, to close pores, bring blood to the surface, increase circulation, tighten skin and leave you feeling invigorated.
- Daily movement.
- Skin brushing.
- Saunas and steams.

- Baths with Epsom salts — start with ½ cup building to 4 cups for 20 minutes.
- Sea salt: detoxifies radiation — up to 1–2 cups per tub.
- Baking soda: makes body more alkaline — ¼ cup per tub.
- Cider vinegar: normalizes skin pH — ½ to 1 cup per tub.

9.3 Luscious Treatment For Your Locks

Every hair on your body is a living piece of you that is growing from a live root that is embedded in your skin at the base of your hair follicle. Your hair, just like your skin and the health of the two, can tell you a lot of what's really going on inside the body.

Ensuring good circulation is provided to your scalp is an important part of having healthy shiny hair. A daily scalp massage will do wonders for getting the right amount of oxygen and nutrient-rich blood to the scalp to feed and nourish your hair.

When choosing a shampoo and conditioner, review the list of ingredients to avoid. You will notice that all body products whether for skin, body, make-up, or hair have similar lists of ingredients. In many types of organic shampoos and conditioners, you will find ingredients such as certified organic tea tree oil. This particular ingredient has been used for a long time to treat a variety of skin conditions, including bites, dandruff, burns, and blisters. Certified organic tea tree oil has antiseptic elements that can aid in controlling naturally occurring microbial levels that can result in different forms of scalp irritation.

Another popular ingredient in many organic shampoo and conditioner products is beta glucan. Beta glucan has immune-enhancing properties both internally and topically. It helps to soothe inflamed cells of the scalp, which is particularly beneficial for people who suffer from skin conditions.

True organic shampoo and conditioner products offer a wealth of benefits for your hair and scalp that will be immediately noticeable. Organic products gently infuse your hair follicles and skin cells with natural minerals, herbal extracts, and oils. If you are looking for shampoos that stimulate healthy hair growth, look for products that are made with aloe vera and coconut oil, as they naturally moisturize your scalp. If you need enhanced shine and moisture for your hair, organic shea butter is an important ingredient to look for in your organic shampoo.

When you use organic shampoos and conditioners, you're also helping your environment by letting biodegradable substances go down the drain instead of harsh chemicals.

Shampoos that I love are Giovanni Tea Tree Shampoo and Conditioner, Burt's Bees, Aubrey Organics, and Suki.

If you have chemically or colour-treated hair, your search for an all-natural option may take a little longer. Talk to your hair stylist and see what they can recommend. If they don't know anything about natural products then please visit your local health store to ask one of their beauty consultants. Also inquire about a more natural selection for your hair colour.

For an inexpensive conditioning hair treatment, use the same avocado recipe described above (for your facemask), or apply a thin coat of your body oil throughout your scalp. For the avocado treatment, cover your hair with a warm towel for 20 to 30 minutes and then wash as per usual. For the oil treatment do this at night, use an old pillowcase to sleep on and when you wake in the morning wash your hair well.

9.4 Don't Forget About Down There ...

This is one area of chatter that definitely raises eyebrows when I bring it up in my workshops and classes ... what do you choose for the oh-so-important personal hygiene? Taboo? Absolutely NOT! Don't you remember what you just finished reading about your skin, all of your skin? It is eating and absorbing all day long! The cells on the inside of your vagina are no exception.

Organic tampons just make sense for something that comes into contact with delicate tissues of your body on a regular basis. It has been estimated that we can use as much as 9,000 tampons in our lifetimes. I thought this was an exaggeration, but do the math. As an example, four tampons for six days, twelve months a year for thirty years is 8,640. That's a lot of tampons and that is a low estimate, it's probably somewhere more like 11,000 ... that's a whole lot of sticks-o-joy (so joking) ladies. ☺

Many women are unaware that rayon and rayon-cotton blends, which we avoid buying in our clothing because of how cheap they are and how poor they wash and wear, are widely used in the manufacture of tampons. Rayon is commonly chlorine-bleached, and is a highly absorbent fibre, which rapidly absorbs menstrual blood but at the same time can also dry out the natural protective mucous lining of the vagina.

Dioxin, a toxic carcinogen, is a by-product of all chlorine bleaching methods and is also found throughout the environment in varying levels as a by-product of pesticide spraying and pollution from incinerators. Dioxin has been found to collect in the fatty tissues of animals, including humans and should, therefore, be a real concern for women. Reports have shown that evidence is growing that even low levels of dioxins may be linked to cancer, endometriosis, low sperm counts and immune system suppression. Considering how many tampons a woman will use in her lifetime, she may be subjecting herself to additional dioxin exposure.

Sometimes I feel like we're in a bit of a chemical shitstorm. Fortunately, if we make better choices, we can eliminate some of the harmful chemicals that have become so much a part of our everyday lives and minimize our risks associated with them.

The brand I love and prefer is Natracare. Their tampons are all made from only certified organic 100 percent cotton and were the world's first fully certified organic cotton tampons. They are non-chlorine bleached and women can be reassured that they do not contain synthetic materials, such as rayon, or chemical additives such as binders or surfactants. Certified organic cotton removes the risk of direct exposure to residues from chemical pesticides and fertilizers used on traditional cotton.

For me, purchasing organic tampons is part of my plan for removing as many unnecessary chemicals as I can for myself, my family, and the environment. Let's see, 8,640 **organic** non-toxic tampons for myself, my daughter, and those that I teach ... now that's a good start.

There is also the DivaCup; it is not for everyone. ☺ There is a bit of a learning curve for this little tool. The DivaCup is a reusable, bell-shaped menstrual cup that is worn internally and sits low in the vaginal canal, collecting rather than absorbing your menstrual flow. Menstrual cups have existed since the 1930s when women were searching for an alternative to the choices of the time. Yet, its breakthrough into the feminine hygiene industry is much more recent.

Their slogan is actually this:

"It goes where? I have to do what? Yes, you wear The DivaCup in "there", in your vagina ... but we promise, it is not as scary

as it sounds. In fact, your body will thank you for giving it the period care it deserves. "[17]

While I can't say I agree with this statement 100%, I can tell you that practice makes using the cup much easier. However, heavy flow days and being out in public washrooms are not good companions to the cup. It can be a bloody mess—no pun intended. ☺

They are a relatively inexpensive investment, that if enjoyed will save you mega bucks on your feminine care products. Whether or not you decide to try the DivaCup is not important. What is important is that you STOP using regular commercial tampons and switch to 100% organic—your body will thank you from the inside out!

9.5 Holistic & Alternative Body Care Treatments

I strongly encourage you to explore and experiment with the amazing array of chiropractic, osteopathy, homeopathy, naturopathic medicine, herbalist, massage therapy, Reiki, energy work, acupuncture, shiatsu treatments that surround you.

We are blessed with many different modalities of therapies and sources of rejuvenation. We, as individuals, all respond differently to any form of treatment, so thank goodness there is MORE THAN ONE WAY about it! Enjoy this 'self-assignment' and let the treatments begin. ☺

CHAPTER 10

LET THE JOURNEY BEGIN

Of all the tools you could choose to adopt as a measurement or way to track your success, and determine the areas you need to continue improving, keeping a journal is probably one of the most profound. By doing this, you will have a foolproof system of back-tracking your choices and pin-pointing the areas to embrace and enhance, and those that you need to change and learn from. Your checklist will provide you a quick reference, so that when in doubt, you can refer back to it to keep you, **OR** get you back on track!

10.1 Your Simplicity Project "On My Way To Feeling Awesome" Checklist

Here is a quick checklist/reference guide to get you through all that you have read to this point. It is a TON of information. I don't argue that for a moment. But, as I have been telling you, everything is connected. There truly is no beginning and no ending. If I only gave you part of the information, then you would only partly understand and only partly achieve your goals.

Your goal is not to attack *your* Simplicity Project right this moment; your goal is to sit down and think about what you have just read, to look at the list below, and start checking off one thing at a time. If you truly want this to be the end of dieting, counting calories, and spending an hour on the treadmill going nowhere fast, then you need to slow down, and let it sink in. As you read through this list and flip back through the pages of this book, connect to the things that resonate most with you. The revelations, points, and suggestions that make the most sense and hit closest to home, the ones that you totally know you can shift right away—this is where you begin.

Everything else will come in time. Once you begin shifting your health in one area, you will be amazed at how strong the trickle effect is into the other areas too. I use this example often: When you begin healthy meals and snacks, you feel great; then you decide to give yourself just one little treat and *whammo,* you are down for the count! The food might taste okay going down, but once the chewing and swallowing has stopped, you will be left with zero energy, a nagging headache, a bloated belly, stinky gas, and a food hangover that sticks around ... it's the not-so-great gift that keeps on giving.

I call it a gift because, once you experience this food hangover effect a few times, you will do this to yourself less and less often—it's just not worth it.

These are by no means the only steps you should be taking; they are merely, as I said, a summary checklist.

- Read the book—Wahoo!
- Complete your Hormonal Health Profile.

- Fill out a sacred contract to yourself.
- Begin journaling, doodling, drawing, and connecting to what you are after.
- Begin to purge the crap! Go through your kitchen cupboards, your fridge, your bathroom, your make-up bag, your feminine products, and your household cleaners. You need to think about detoxing the whole shebang!
- Connect to and notice HOW your food is making you FEEL.
- Cut out the digestive system "delinquents" a.k.a. anything that makes you feel lethargic, bloated, gassy, moody, emotional, puffy, constipated, or gives you diarrhoea.
- Toss the junk! Anything that is processed, refined, autolysed, hydrolysed, has white sugar, hydrogenated oil, high fructose corn syrup, and MSG, and stop drinking cow's milk and switch to milk alternatives such as almond, coconut, hemp, flax, or rice.
- No SOY!!!
- Begin your day with a mug half-full of warm water, and add fresh lemon and a tbsp of raw honey or maple syrup.
- Eat within one hour of waking.
- Eat smaller, balanced meals every three to four hours. These should be made up of real food, including a carb, protein and fat at each meal.
- You need to see at least three different colours on your plate and in your bowl.
- Chew more fresh fruits and vegetables.
- Make a daily smoothie and/or fresh juice.

- Drink two litres of water daily. Stop using plastic bottles; they are seriously messing up your thyroid! Choose glass or stainless steel.

- Drink no more than one cup of coffee or black tea daily. Choose herbal teas.

- Drink Kombucha, a fermented tea loaded with probiotics, if not every day, at least four times per week. Your gut will love you for it.

- Stop eating within three hours of going to bed.

- Sleep in light clothing to keep your core body temperature down at night.

- Journal, draw, doodle, get frisky, ☺ or meditate before you sleep.

- Sleep in complete darkness and turn off the lights, TV, cell phones, and computers by 10:00 p.m. to 10:30 p.m. Best sleep is attained between 10:30 p.m. and 6:00 a.m. to 6:30 a.m.

- Exercise for thirty to sixty-minutes five to six days per week: strength train twice weekly, yoga twice weekly, cardio twice weekly.

- Exercise is wonderful, but over-exercising can also stress your thyroid and over-stimulate your adrenal glands, elevating your cortisol levels, so take it easy Cardio Queen. ☺

- Counter your daily stress. There are many ways—some requiring more of a commitment than others—to help your body relax. From yoga to walking to deep breathing exercises to scheduling a massage or day at the spa, you always have options.

- Teach your heart, belly, and liver to smile. ☺ ☺ ☺

- Throw out all of your cosmetics, body products, and regular feminine hygiene products that are laden with chemicals, parabens, sodium laureate sulfate, PEG 70, perfumes, dyes, etc., and your average and most popular commercial brand name body care products you are buying. They are a pure chemical shit storm and are MASSIVELY affecting not only your thyroid but EVERY SINGLE CELL in your body. I cannot stress this enough.

- Moms, get your children off these commercial products. Do you want them to ever have to feel how you feel right now?

- Add a daily probiotic supplement, vitamin D 2000 IU, omega 3 fatty acids, fish oil, a complete B complex with extra vitamin B12, 2000 mcg. in sublingual form, vitamin C—two packages of Emergen C.

- Additional supplements and/or herbs may be recommended based on a personal consultation with a qualified practitioner.

- Consult your family doctor, or better yet a naturopathic doctor, to get your blood levels tested properly. Always ask for a copy of your blood work.

- If you need medication, discuss this with a naturopath as there may be ways to use bio-identical hormones or more natural forms of medication to help you and not harm you.

- Remember to take one thing at a time!

- PLAN! PLAN! PLAN!

- Before you head to the grocery store, create a meal plan asking each family member to choose one meal for the week.

- Celebrate the small steps you make along the way. More water today ... awesome! More veggies today ... amazing! You exercised for thirty minutes and didn't hate it ... right on!

10.2 **Food Journal**

Name: _____ Date: _____

Temperature (upon rising): _____

(this will help to determine optimal thyroid function)

FOOD & DRINK	TIME	Here is a list of everything I ate and drank today (including tiny bites). *Please indicate approximate amounts.*
Pre-breakfast		
Breakfast		
Snack (mid-morning)		
Lunch		
Snack (mid-afternoon)		
Dinner		
Snack (evening)		

Medications / Supplements / Herbs / Other		

What did you notice (physically, mentally) after eating any of the above foods?

_____

_____

_____

Water Intake:

☐ ☐ ☐ ☐ ☐ ☐ ☐ ☐ ☐ ☐ cups (250 ml in one cup)

Digestion:

Number of bowel movements: _____

Description (size, colour, undigested food, etc.):

_____

Other observations (gas/bloating, burping, acid stomach, etc.):

_____

Cravings for: ☐ salty   ☐ sweet   ☐ spicy   ☐ chocolate

☐ coffee   ☐ starches (breads, donuts, etc.)

Energy Level:

(low energy) 1   2   3   4   5   6   7   8   9   10 (high energy)

Stress Level:

(low stress) 1   2   3   4   5   6   7   8   9   10 (high stress)

Mood(s) & Emotion(s):

How would you describe your mood(s) today?

_____

Was there a time when your mood changed today? What happened?

_____

Exercise: (number of minutes/type of exercise)

_____

What are you GRATEFUL for today?

_____

Remember that the most successful people, whether at losing weight, committing to exercise, running a 10 km, living their lives more fully, or changing the eating habits they've had for a lifetime, all have one thing in common: they never stop learning, growing, shifting, and trying to do better! You are going to experience slips, you are going to have crappy days, you are going to ask yourself why the heck are you doing this. I like to call them having "human moments." They are real, they are raw, and they are part of the process that will teach you wonderful things. Enjoy the journey!

Jenn xo

SELECT BIBLIOGRAPHY

Carr, Kris, and Rory Freedman. *Crazy Sexy Diet*. Connecticut: Skirt!, 2011.

Dupont, Caroline. *The New Enlightened Eating: simple recipes for extraordinary living*. Summertown: Book Publishing Company, 2012.

Hay, Louise. *Heal Your Body*. London: Hay House, 1984.

Hyman, Mark. *The Blood Sugar Solution*. USA: Your Coach In A Box, 2012.

Mercola, Joseph. "Dr. Mercola on Natural Health Products & Articles." http://www.drmercola.com/.

Organic Beauty Talk. "Ingredients to Avoid." http://www.organicbeautytalk.com/ingredients-to-avoid/.

Oz, Mehmet C., and Michael F. Roizen. *YOU: On A Diet Revised Edition: The Owner's Manual for Waist Management*. New York: Simon & Schuster, Inc., 2009.

Pang, Kenny. "The Thyroid Specialist." http://www.thethyroiddoctor.com/.

Perrault, Danielle. *Nutritional Symptomatology: A Handbook for CSNN Students*. Canada: Canadian School of Natural Nutrition, 2001.

Rubin, Alan L. *Diabetes For Dummies, 3rd Edition.* Canada: Wiley Publishing, 2008.

Turner, Natasha. *The Hormone Diet.* Canada: Random House, 2009.

NOTES

1. Natasha Turner, *The Hormone Diet* (Canada: Random House, 2009), 38.

2. Ibid., 85, 300, 381.

3. Phyllis A. Balch, *Prescription For Nutritional Healing* (London: Penguin Group, 2006), 502-503.

4. Danielle Perrault, *A Handbook for CSNN Students* (Canada: Canadian School of Natural Nutrition, 2001), 25–26.

5. "Cut down on the overtime!," Mail Online, publication September 11, 2012, http://www.dailymail.co.uk/ health/article-2201519/Working-hours-day-raises-risk-heart-disease-80.html.

6. "Chemical Cuisine, Learn about Food Additives," Center for Science in the Public Interest, http://www.cspinet. org/reports/chemcuisine.htm.

7. "EWG's 2012 Shopper's Guide to Pesticides in Produce™," last modified June 19, 2012, http://www. ewg.org/foodnews/summary/.

8. "Tower Garden," http://www.towergarden.com.

9. "EWG's 2012 Shopper's Guide to Pesticides in Produce™," last modified June 19, 2012, http://www. ewg.org/foodnews/summary/.

10. "How much sugar does the average person consume every year?" Sharecare, http://www.sharecare.com/question/sugar-consume-every-year.

11. "Aspartame is, by Far, the Most Dangerous Substance on the Market that is Added To Foods," published November 6, 2011, http://articles.mercola.com/sites/articles/archive/2011/11/06/aspartame-most-dangerous-substance-added-to-food.aspx.

12. "Sucralose," on Whole Foods Market website, http://www.wholefoodsmarket.com/healthinfo/sucralose.html (page discontinued).

13. "More Chronic Cardio Talk," Mark's Daily Apple, http://www.marksdailyapple.com/chronic-cardio-2/#axzz2JQBijmHr.

14. Jenn Pike, "Yoga Sequences," http://www.youtube.com/user/JennPikes?feature-mhee

15. "Ingredients to Avoid," Organic Beauty Talk, http://www.organicbeautytalk.com/ingredients-to-avoid/.

16. Ibid.

17. "The DivaCup," http://divacup.com/products/the-divacup/.

PERMISSIONS

Every attempt has been made to give proper acknowledgement, and access appropriate permissions for quotes. Any oversights are purely unintentional. In the unlikely event something has been missed, please accept our regret and apology, and contact us immediately so we can investigate and rectify as needed.

PUBLISHER'S NOTE

Jenn's brilliance is her ability to take a ton of information, find the truths within, add to it her own vast knowledge and experience, and turn it into something that we all can understand and actually use in our own lives. Not only do we feel her passion in every word, her conversational, down-to-earth and humorous style of writing engages us from beginning to end. We know that we too, can use *The Simplicity Project* to lead us to optimum health and well-being.

As publisher and editor of *The Simplicity Project*, Jenn was a joy to work with. Her hard work and dedication were instrumental in bringing this project to fruition. I look forward to seeing more from this motivating and inspirational author in the future.

Sheri Andrunyk
Publisher, Editor, Author, Speaker & Consultant
Insightful Communications Publishing
I C Publishing ... Committed to Quality Content

For info about special discounts for bulk purchases, please go to ICpublishing.ca.

Should you be interested in booking our dynamic authors/ speakers for your events or media interviews, please contact info@icpublishing.ca.